Classics in Youth Cultural Studies

Maurizio Merico

# Classics in Youth Cultural Studies

**PETER LANG**

Lausanne - Berlin - Bruxelles - Chennai - New York - Oxford

Library of Congress Cataloging-in-Publication Data
A CIP catalog record for this book has been applied for at the
Library of Congress.

**Bibliographic Information published by the
Deutsche Nationalbibliothek**
The Deutsche Nationalbibliothek lists this publication in the
Deutsche Nationalbibliografie; detailed bibliographic data is
available online at http://dnb.d-nb.de.

Published with the contribution of the
Department of Political and Social Studies of the University of Salerno

ISBN 978-3-631-89485-9 (Print)
E-ISBN 978-3-631-89507-8 (E-PDF)
E-ISBN 978-3-631-89508-5 (EPUB)
DOI 10.3726/b20486

© 2023 Peter Lang Group AG, Lausanne
Published by:
Peter Lang GmbH, Berlin, Deutschland

info@peterlang.com - www.peterlang.com

All rights reserved.

All parts of this publication are protected by copyright. Any
utilisation outside the strict limits of the copyright law, without
the permission of the publisher, is forbidden and liable to
prosecution. This applies in particular to reproductions,
translations, microfilming, and storage and processing in
electronic retrieval systems.

# Table of Contents

Introduction .................................................................................................. 7

### 1  Youth in the city. Looking back to the Chicago School of Sociology ............................................................................................. 15
    1.1.  The city as a social laboratory ................................................... 15
    1.2.  Living the interstices .................................................................. 18
    1.3.  Mapping juvenile delinquency ................................................. 22
    1.4.  Young women ............................................................................. 26
    1.5.  Motion pictures and youth ....................................................... 30
    1.6.  Looking back to Chicago ........................................................... 35

### 2  Youth and generations. Background, contents and (in)actuality of Karl Mannheim's perspective ................................. 37
    2.1.  An outdated concept? ................................................................ 37
    2.2.  The sociological "problem of generations" ............................ 38
    2.3.  Generations and social change ................................................. 42
    2.4.  Youth as outsiders ...................................................................... 47
    2.5.  Critical aspects ........................................................................... 51
    2.6.  An open-ended debate .............................................................. 55

### 3  Youth culture and the peer group. Looping back around to Talcott Parsons ................................................................................ 57
    3.1.  The peer group and the transition to adulthood ................... 57
    3.2.  The "psychosocial moratorium" .............................................. 61
    3.3.  Youth culture and social integration ....................................... 63

    3.4. An "adolescent society"? ............................................................. 65

    3.5. Youth culture and the value system ............................................. 69

    3.6. Between sociological analysis and "myth" ................................... 73

## 4 Youth, dissent and counterculture. The "long 1960s" in Goodman, Keniston, and Roszak ........................................................ 79

    4.1. The (un)complacent youth ............................................................ 79

    4.2. "Growing up absurd"? Paul Goodman's visionary sociology ............... 81

    4.3. Faces of dissent: From youth alienation to youth protest ................... 84

    4.4. Roszak and "The Making of a Counter Culture" ............................. 90

    4.5. A "postmodern youth" .................................................................. 94

    4.6. Fury, symbol, value ....................................................................... 97

## 5 Rituals, resistance and style. The CCCS and youth subcultures ................................................................................................ 99

    5.1. A new research agenda ................................................................. 99

    5.2. Theoretical foundations ............................................................... 101

    5.3. "Resistance through rituals" ......................................................... 104

    5.4. The meaning of style ................................................................... 107

    5.5. Homology and creativity .............................................................. 111

    5.6. From symbolic challenges to incorporations ................................. 115

    5.7. Subcultures and beyond .............................................................. 117

**References** ........................................................................................... 121

# Introduction

Social research on young people has been widely recognised as both consistent and relevant. Between the late 1970s and the early 1980s a specialised field of study progressively took shape, gaining full legitimacy and recognition within the social sciences (Furlong, 2013; Côté, 2014; Ibrahim & Steinberg, 2014; Wyn & Cahill, 2015; Kelly & Kamp, 2015). In the perspective embraced herein, the field of youth studies is intrinsically interdisciplinary, despite boasting a strong sociological core.

Nowadays, many practitioners, experts and specialists falling under youth studies understand the field as having two dominant pillars (perspectives or "twin tracks"): the first bringing together studies that, despite their heterogeneity, focus on transitions (in particular on the transition to adulthood); the second encompassing studies and research hinging on a cultural perspective and examining various youth cultural forms (Woodman & Bennett, 2015a). This distinction offers a useful analytical framework to classify and systematise the wide range of studies on young people that is currently available, both at the national and international levels. Moreover, it allows to pinpoint the differences – in terms of interpretation categories, methodological orientations and reference contexts – between the studies and research projects inspired by one or the other perspective respectively (Cohen, 1997; Furlong, Woodman & Wyn, 2011).

Despite sharing their foundational premises, "there are […] many studies that do resemble one approach more than the other and orient to the different canonical texts and to the latest debates within either the transitions or cultures approach" (Woodman & Bennett, 2015a: 2). This polarisation has been affected by the ways in which scientific and academic research has defined itself in the past decades, firstly in terms of organisation, and then as regards funding structure and editorial politics. This process has led to a progressive and pervasive specialisation and segmentation of youth research – culminating in a representation of the relationship of the two traditions as deeply fragmented and marred by tensions and hostility.

Nevertheless, if one looks closely, that between "transition" and "cultural" perspectives appears to be a false binary, abating the possibility of a comprehensive, far-reaching and holistic understanding of youth in modern societies. This becomes particularly clear in late modern contexts, where the complexity within which young people build and give meaning to their lives and experiences necessarily calls for a re-consideration of the interlinkages, interdependencies and connections between the structural and cultural dimensions (Woodman & Bennett, 2015b). Only in this way can we better understand both the specific aspects giving shape to "transitions" and those lending meaning to "cultures", as well as the differences and convergences between the two research areas.

In light of this, the book chooses as object of analysis those which are currently defined as *"youth cultural studies"*, to retrace the main steps of the process leading to the emergence and the consolidation of this perspective within youth studies. The exploration of the *Classics in youth cultural studies* commences with a dive into the analytical pathway developed by the Chicago School of Sociology in the 1920s and 1930s and comes to a close with the research on youth subcultures conducted by the Birmingham Centre for Contemporary Cultural Studies. Along the way are Mannheim's reflections on the *crisis* riddling Europe between the two World Wars; the studies on "youth culture" carried out in the United States around the 1940s and 1950s; and the re-evaluation of some contributions to the debate on youth dissent and student protest.

The ultimate aim is that of rebuilding the corpus of theoretical and methodological approaches, themes of analysis and interpretation categories, contexts for reflection and orientations that – in their intrinsic and much-needed articulation – constitute the "paradigm" (Cristofori, 1997) from which contemporary research on youth cultures originates and upon which it rests (Bennett, 2016). This corpus is the result of a long process of accumulation, subtraction and crystallisation of observations, analyses, interpretations and knowledge able to collectively give shape to a tradition and body of science. As Jon Elster (1989) put it, these are the *Nuts and Bolts* making up the toolbox of the youth researcher to which those who practice or are interested in social research, can resort to interpret and comprehend key matters in the debate on young people and youth cultures.

At a time when the analytical relevance of the concept of "youth culture" is being questioned, we staunchly believe that going back to reading the *Classics* is not (and should not be) a mere stylistic exercise, nor should it correspond to the callous celebration of an academic ritual. It represents a decisive moment to return "to existing, if undervalued alternatives for thinking about youth" and "rework in imaginative ways the theoretical resources already widely used in youth studies" (Woodman & Bennett, 2015b: 190), in order to (re)affirm the value and validity of the concept (Bourdieu, 1984) and consequently give new and more vigorous recognition to the perspective of *"youth cultural studies"* (Bennett, 2015). This legitimation must be explicitly based – to draw on previous considerations – on theories and methodologies that strive to avoid the risks of remaining trapped "within a conceptual model that distinguishes between structural, historically specific conditions and young people's subjective experience of the times in which they live" (Furlong, Woodman & Wyn, 2011: 360). This is, in our view, the main contribution offered by the exploration of the *Classics in youth cultural studies*, which Andy Furlong (2015: 17) has clearly explicated: "For many of the most eminent youth researchers, culture and transition are lenses, starting points, and researchers working outward from these positions work freely across what is rightly regarded as a false binary". As we will see in the next chapters, each form of legitimation of *"youth cultural studies"* must inevitably rest on the need to be open to further expansion: namely on the ability to recognise the complexity and intrinsic multiplicity of the phenomena studied; on the readiness, as argued by Sheila Allen (1968), to engage in dialogue with heterogeneous approaches and perspectives without settling for predefined standpoints, and last but not least, on the awareness of the necessity for an open and concurrently deep outlook.

From the privileged – yet by no means exclusive – vantage point of sociology, the book contributes to retracing the pathway leading to the elaboration of the corpus of tradition and knowledge that makes up contemporary youth cultural studies. It thus goes back and revisits landmark moments in research on youth cultures, which are emblematic of an objectively broader and more articulated experience. In this sense, it is important to clarify that the book is not designed to lay out the "history" of social research on youth cultures. It does not purport to be complete or exhaustive. Rather, in the words of Italian anthropologist Ernesto de Martino (1961), the five analytical pathways presented and discussed herein are to be understood as "molecular" contributions serving to delineate the origins and the development of research on youth cultures. The reflections conducted for each of the *Classics in youth cultural studies* presented can thus be conceived as "conversations" that remain purposely open (Berger, 1963a), so as to offer the reader the opportunity to engage in dialogue with the different analytical perspectives encountered in the volume.

The overall organisation of the book is inspired by the attempt to turn back to the objects of study, the questions and themes of reflection, the perspectives of analysis, the interpretation categories and tools of investigation that were gradually developed giving rise to a field of study and research specifically devoted to the examination of youth cultures. The selection of each "classic" in *youth cultural studies* was influenced by two factors. The first links back to the possibility of identifying a periodisation – doubtless flexible and fluid – for research on youth and youth cultures (Helve & Holm, 2005; Côté, 2014), thus segmenting the overall trajectory examined as a collection of *phases*, each characterised, as Tamara K. Hareven (1976) intuitively remarked, by the distinct perception of youth as socially problematic (Cicchelli & Merico, 2001; Merico, 2004). The second element – clearly influenced by the sensitivity of those tasked with making the selection – relates to the ability of each of the pathways identified to encapsulate the themes, categories, questions, ideas and interpretation models that over time have enriched the sociological and social sciences debate (Kett, 2003; Furlong, 2013; Cieslik & Simpson, 2013). In short, while not including all potential contributions, the five analytical pathways contained in this book can be considered as emblematic of the emergence and entrenchment, in each of the phases outlined above, of a new point of view and outlook – spearheaded by adults, institutions, research – on young people and youth cultures (Becker, 2008).

The five pathways discussed in the book, which follow one another yet occasionally overlap, are a testament to the overarching trajectory of social research on youth cultures, and speak to the emergence, consolidation and surpassing of specific interpretation models. Our interpretation is that this trajectory represents in many ways a parabola: it opens up at first when recognising a privileged relationship between youth and urban modernity (Fass, 1977), as well as in relation to its gradual identification – as per the terminology used by the Chicago School – as "social problem". Then, the generational dynamic and the specific sociological function of youth, conceived by Karl Mannheim as "latent resource" for socio-cultural change, is recognised. The following steps coincide with the recognition by Parsons' structural-functionalism of "youth culture" as a specific analytical category holding great sociological value. This conceptualisation has maintained widespread evocative potential over time, taking on a leading role in social research. Nonetheless, it is the normative dimension undergirding the definition which has paved the way for its critical revisitation, starting from the "mythical" dimensions of the category and subsequently focusing on the theme of "dissent" as manifested by youth in the 1970s. The last step of the journey is rooted in the spectacular outburst of subcultures spearheaded by young people hailing from the British working class: an analysis, that beyond its specific contents, allows to fully grasp the intrinsically controversial nature and the much-need ductility of the theorisations, approaches and concepts used in research on young people (Dimitriadis, 2008; Jones, 2009; Lesko & Talburt, 2012).

The five chapters thus present the historical and theoretical premises of each analytical perspective considered, the contents of the elaboration suggested by the scholars who have influenced their systematisation, their internal articulation, critical issues of greater importance and contributions that continue to remain current. What follows is a short summary of the key contents.

Looking back at the profound congruence between the urban dimension and the experiences of the new generations in the United States at the start of the last century, Chapter 1 reviews the main research studies on youth and youth cultures carried out by the Chicago School of Sociology, inspired by the analytical approach developed by Robert E. Park, Ernest W. Burgess and William I. Thomas. Crediting Jane Addams' and other *Hull House* activists' for their pioneering contribution – which for a long time was regrettably, largely ignored – the Chapter outlines the social typologies that best embody the contradictions afflicting the presence of youth in Chicago's "social laboratory": hobos, youth living in the slums, gangs, the so-called "unadjusted" girls and taxi-dance halls dancers. It delves deeper into the examination of juvenile delinquency made by Shaw and McKay at the *Institute of Juvenile Research* and the contribution by Blumer, Thrasher and Cressey to the analysis of the relationship between motion pictures and youth, as part of the Payne Fund Studies.

Chapter 2 offers a reflection on the background, contents and (in)actuality of Karl Mannheim's perspective. In particular, two essays are discussed: the first is "Das Problem der Generationen" ("The problem of generations"), one of his most popular works, commonly considered as the first sociological systematisation of the concept of generation. In the second part of the Chapter we discuss, instead, "The Problem of Youth in Modern Society", a rather unknown text, presented by Mannheim at various conferences held in the 1940s in England. The joint examination of the two works allows to flesh out the main aspects of his thinking and grasp the role he credited generations in the social and cultural process of change, the sociological function he ascribed to young people, and finally, the excerpts of this work that are still useful to the study of youth cultures.

The broad debate which took shape between the 1940s and 1950s around the possibility of recognising, first and foremost in the American context, the distinctive features of a "youth culture" is the focus of Chapter 3. The reflection presented draws on Talcott Parsons' interpretation, accompanied by references to the works of Kinsley Davis and Samuel N. Eisenstadt, to the category of "psychosocial moratorium" put forward by Erik H. Erikson, up until the contributions made by Kinsley Davis, James S. Coleman and by Fred and Grace Hechinger. In their variety, the analyses carried out by these scholars bear witness to the profound ambivalence which characterises, in the period examined, the role of the peer group and of youth culture, understood as causes of the potential rise of an "adolescent society", on the one hand, or as "safety valve" enabling the transition to adulthood, on the other.

Retracing the main events affecting young people's lives in the "long 1960s", Chapter 4 teases out the themes of youth dissent, student protest and the birth of the so-called youth counterculture. More specifically, it examines the works of Paul Goodman, Theodore Roszak and – albeit in more detail – Kenneth Keniston: three intellectuals and scholars with different theoretical and disciplinary backgrounds, sharing a sympathy towards those dissenting young people and the transformation potential they embody. The result is a trajectory that allows to rebuild the premises, the multiple faces, the more immediate outcomes and consequences of one of the periods of maximum visibility and enkindling of youth protagonism. In the final part of the Chapter, we turn to the hypothesis put forward by Keniston in relation to the identification of peculiar traits of "postmodern youth": namely that generation witnessing the emergence of a new style and the profound transformation in the organisation of the life course, which gradually became a key reference in subsequent decades.

The last of the *Classics* discussed in the book concerns the work on youth subcultures carried out by scholars collaborating with Stuart Hall at the Centre for Contemporary Cultural Studies at Birmingham University. After laying out its theoretical backdrop, Chapter 5 first focuses on *Resistance through rituals*: it thus highlights both the attempt made by researchers belonging to the "Subcultures Group" to (re)kindle the attention given to "class" in studies on young people, and the features of their interpretation, characterised by the importance attributed to the cultural perspective. More generally, the focus on the works of Hall, Clarke, Hebdige, Willis and other researchers hailing from the Centre offers the opportunity to trace the boundaries of an ethnographic exploration that recognises in the rituals enacted by young people of the working class a form of resistance that offers a symbolic "solution" to the problems deriving from their social positions and outlines the peculiarities of the style adopted, the homologies influencing its elaboration, the creativity it expresses, as well as the attempts to tame its oppositional force of resistance.

In its specificity, each of the *Classics in youth cultural studies* included in the book offer a peculiar image (or a collection of images) of the way of studying, understanding and representing youth cultures, that is the expression, time and again, of a different theoretical or methodological approach, of specific historical, social and cultural conditions, as well as of a new relationship between generations (Griffin, 1993). At the same time, there are two elements, closely intertwined and cross-cutting to all the pathways examined, that testify to the most evident peculiarities undergirding, as we mentioned in our opening, the definition of the research tradition on youth cultures. The first element concerns the specific attention given to change: a theme that has regularly accompanied social research on young people (Passerini, 1997; Furlong, Woodman & Wyn,

2011; Merico & Morciano, 2017), to which, as we will see, each of the contributions analysed in the book turns to, thereby reconfirming once again, its essential role. The second element links back to the ambivalence – Howard S. Becker (2008) would call it the "paradox" – that has historically clouded the human gaze (of adults, institutions, and as far as we are concerned, social research) on young people and their cultural expression. A gaze that Luisa Passerini (1997) has claimed recalls the mythological two-faced Janus. We will find it systematically across the five chapters: in the intersection between "romance and mystery [...], comedy and tragedy" typical of the urban life of young people in Chicago (Thrasher, 1927[2]: 3); in the reactions to the "latent resource" manifested by the young generations studied by Mannheim; in the tension between deviance and conformism that accompanies studies on "youth culture" from the 1940s and 1950s; in the continuum between alienation and commitment, complacency and protest, characterising the relationship between youth and dissent in the long 1960s; up until the spectacular rise of subcultures, negotiating rituals, styles and attempts to subsume them.

Retracing the peculiar traits of the experiences of young people of the roaring 1920s, in *The Damned and the Beautiful* the American historian Paula S. Fass (1977) explicitly refers to Francis Scott Fitzgerald's novel (1922), pointing to the dominant interpretation employed with regard to young people: represented at times as "angels", at times as "demons" (Austin & Willard, 1998); understood in ways as trouble (problematic subjects to control and punish), in ways as resources (bearers of innovation, who ought to be supported and empowered) (Williamson, 2017). This ambivalence is part and parcel of our analysis, as it allows us to describe a field of study – the one on youth cultures – characterised by an intrinsic "tension". This tension exists between disciplines, because while the overarching approach rests on sociology – as does this book – it also opens up to anthropology, psychology, education studies and even cultural studies (Dimitriadis, 2008). The tension can also be noticed between variables and dimensions that are progressively evoked by the analysis: age, gender, class, ethnic origin, etc. (Cohen, 1997). There is also a tension between interpretation categories: to mention but a few relevant ones in the approaches examined, "social problem" and "interstices", "generations", "youth culture", "opposition" and "dissent", "subcultures". It is a tension that more generally underpins the overlap and succession of profoundly different theoretical and methodological approaches.

Finally, it is a tension that necessarily accompanies, in the past and today, social research on a subject of study – youth cultures – that by its very nature is malleable, dynamic, in constant evolution. This is a time when research on young people is witnessing further expansion and consolidation, but runs the risk of losing the relationship with its own background and memory. For this reason, the opportunity, and perhaps the need arises to diligently re-consider the premises, contents, limits and potential developments of the analyses that have marked the tradition. This is essential to grasp – this is our hope – their pressing actuality and the inspirations that they are still able to offer today.

# 1 Youth in the city. Looking back to the Chicago School of Sociology

## 1.1. The city as a social laboratory

From its very inception, the Chicago School of Sociology placed special attention on the urban dimension, intended – as per Albion Small's definition – as a *social laboratory* (Park, 1929). The Chicago School of Sociology set out to examine the dynamics that underlie the urban dimension, starting from the study of its spatial layout. Back then, the city was perceived as a radically new world that challenged the traditional practices and conventions of rural communities, and at the same time constantly called itself into question due to the incessant mobility of urban life. This realisation gave rise to a vast collection of research studies on "urbanism as a way of life" (Wirth, 1938), which delve deeper into the various forms of social organisation and their relationship with the physical structure of the city, communication processes, social control, commercialised vice and crime (Park, 1915).

Young people rapidly became among the chief research subjects of the Chicago School. This was a result of the fact that, as argued by Frederic M. Thrasher (1927[2]: 3), their relationship with the city was one of interplay between "comedy and tragedy", where one could discern "the romance and mystery of a great city", its "unvarnished emotions", opportunities and risks, and the hopes and the fears that American society nurtured towards the new generations (Bennett, 1981).

In the midst of this, urban life offered young people "new modes of associations and new kinds of human connections around a wide range of tastes, dispositions, and lifestyles" (Dimitriadis, 2008: 26), able to engender novel forms and ways of acting and thinking, new languages, codes, and guiding schemas. In turn, the analysis of young people's daily lives, their experiences, behavioural models, desires and practices offered a privileged vantage point from which to observe the ongoing erosion of traditional social control mechanisms and the development of new forms of social (re)organisation (Thomas, 1921[2]). In fact, as David Nasaw pointed out ever so aptly, "the early twentieth-century city was a city of strangers. Most of its inhabitants had been born or raised elsewhere. Only the children were native to the city" (Nasaw, 1985[2]: 195). These individuals grew hand in hand with the city and the city grew hand in hand with them: the city of electric lights, streetcars, department stores, skyscrapers, the telephone, movies, work and leisure (D'Eramo, 2003). This city was literally "the only world they knew" and children and young people were both more prepared and suited to soak it all in (Nasaw, 1985[2]: vii).

This novelty fuelled the "transformation of ideas about, institutions for, and social experiences" of young people (Kett, 2003: 371). It further encouraged a range of professionals – education assistants, social settlement residents, social workers, the judiciary and playground volunteers – to initiate a systematic process of observation of the relationship between young people and urban reality (Platt, 1969[2]; Solomon, 2005). Departing from the acknowledgement that "social progress required a synthesis of study and action, science and social reform", a knowledge-gathering process, largely external to academia, was initiated (Condliffe Lagemann, 1994: x). It's role was of de facto anticipating the emergence of the themes, categories of analysis and methods of investigation that irreversibly shaped Chicago's social research.

A clear example of this process is the work developed by the women affiliated with the *Hull House*. Alongside their engagement in designing and implementing some of the leading reforms on childhood and youth, *Hull House* activists and reformers doubtless contributed to a large extent to instigating, at the turn of the century, scientific scrutiny around the realities of younger generations (Deegan, 1988[2]). Aside from the collection of *Hull-House maps and papers* (Residents of Hull-House, 1895), prominent examples include: Florence Kelley's lifelong commitment to ending child labour and related legislation (Kelley, 1889, 1905); Julia Lathrop's role as President of the Juvenile Psychopathic Institute and, since 1912, her appointment as first Chief of the United States Children's Bureau; Edith Abbott and Sophonisba P. Breckinridge's studies on child delinquency and school truancy (Abbott & Breckinridge, 1912, 1917); and in particular, the work of the two *Hull House* co-founders, Ellen Gates Starr and Jane Addams – the latter being the sociologist who published, in 1909, *The spirit of youth and the city streets* and was awarded the Nobel Peace Prize in 1931.

Addams' main aim was to underline how governing institutions were oblivious to the life of youth in the city's streets, and turned a blind eye to the decisive role that play had traditionally covered in young people's development processes – a topic, which was exceptionally dear to Georg H. Mead (Nasaw, 1985[2]). Following an approach that was favoured by several Chicago youth researchers, her narrative was replete with accounts of the (life) stories collected thanks to her engagement in the social settlement. The result was a depiction in which Jane Addams (1909: 45–47) highlighted how boys and girls were in a position to be "made safe only through their own self-control" and "the great processes of social life develop themselves through influences of which each participant is unconscious as he struggles alone and unaided in the strength of a current which seizes him and bears him along". It was thus necessary to actively contribute to defining "juster social conditions" able to preserve what she defined as a "splendid store of youthful ardor and creative enthusiasm" (*Ivi*: 143, 145).

A large part of Jane Addams' theoretical groundwork and research were subsequently almost entirely dismissed by "*the men of the Chicago School*" (Deegan, 1988[2]). Nevertheless, while embracing a perspective that conceptualised in a profoundly different way the relationship between research and reform, Chicago researchers were conscious that "when old habits break down [...] there is always a period of confusion until new habits are established". In other words, they were blatantly aware of the fact that "the demoralization of young persons, the prevalence of delinquency, crime [...] are very serious problems" calling for the pursuit of greater knowledge (Thomas & Thomas, 1928: xiii). For these and others reasons, the majority of research studies devoted to the lived experiences of young people conducted by Chicago researchers focused on relationships and organised interaction – delinquency, commercialised vice, free time, cinema – and on those subjects – hobos, second generation immigrants, members of urban youth gangs, the so-called "unadjusted girl", youth living in the slums – allowing to grasp "the textual richness of the city" and shed light on the rise of social problems (Salerno, 2007: 32).

The underlying objective was thus of understanding how social disorder, mobility, interethnic living, shifts in social control, educational processes, the commercialised organisation of leisure and delinquency affected the behaviour of young people. All this departing from a fundamental theoretical standpoint: the awareness that people's behaviour could not be interpreted – in contrast with what G. Stanley Hall (1904) had posited – in individual and/or biological terms. On the contrary, it had to be analysed in relation to the distinct features of the urban dimension, devoting special attention to the multitude social and cultural contexts in which it unfolded (Getis, 1998).

Accordingly, the analysis developed by the Department of Sociology presented a range of other distinctive features (Getis, 2000). In the first place, a theoretical frame centred on the study of social processes viewed through the lens of *ecological theory* (Park, Burgess & McKenzie, 1925[3]) and social transformation interpreted through the *disorganisation theory* (Thomas & Znaniecki, 1918/1920). In the second place, a systematic reflection on methods and an unprecedented propensity toward empirical research. The latter typically exhibited two core elements: a methodology based on case studies, the production of maps and the analysis of personal documents (Burgess, 1929); and the direct engagement of students, soon-to-be graduates and doctoral students, ushered by Park – in the light of his journalism background – to carry out first hand observation and "go get the seat of [… their] pants dirty in real research" (quoted in Bulmer, 1984: 97). Finally, the institutionalisation of forms of cooperation with civic and social agencies, able to offer young researchers the necessary financial support to conduct their studies and attain a high level of education (White, 1929).

Bearing all this in mind, in the next pages we will revisit the main research carried out by the Chicago School of Sociology on the topic of young people, in an attempt to flesh out its contribution to the definition of the research focus, as well as the theoretical frameworks and empirical tools employed.

## 1.2. Living the interstices

Published in 1923, Nels Anderson's *The Hobo. The sociology of the homeless man* was the first monograph to come out of the University of Chicago *Sociological Series* – a seminal and pioneering work that used participant observation as a research method to reveal the features of urban areas and realities.

Drawing on his own experience of homelessness, via a complex "constellation of human vignettes" (Salerno, 2007: 114), Anderson described the life of a hobo in his natural environment, namely in the "savage neighbourhood" of the city, the slum: that social milieu that surrounded him, yet was also alien to him. The outcome was an analytical approach that gave voice to a largely ignored underclass, describing the biographical and intellectual life, the customs, language, songs and morals of a body of human beings who, for widely varying reasons, chose to define their experience as one of constant openness towards mobility and vagrant life.

In the third part of the book, Anderson dedicated a brief, yet in-depth analysis, to the practices charactering the socialisation of young people living in hobohemia: a process in which promiscuity and violence seem to prevail, together with a sort of "slavery" linked to the need of accepting adults' "perversion".

In a subsequent essay specifically unpacking the relationship between *The juvenile and the tramp*, Anderson (1923/1924) estimated that out of 2 million tramps living in the United States, at that point in time, a quarter were boys under twenty-one: mostly, these were individuals who were less settled than adults and more prone to movement and change. He described different types of boy tramps: the wanderlust, the egocentric, the mentally defective type, the home trouble and the migrant worker. As is apparent in the interviews and materials collected in the summer of 1921, their stories clearly showed the ambivalence typical of the lives of those young people, balancing escape and settling down, work and leisure, social control and access to support. They were intimately enveloped in vice and immorality, yet were also craving "a background of adventure":

> The boy [...] sees in the life on the road a charm and fascination that no other offers. [...] It is a life in which there are no daily tasks and no chores; it is a promise of escape from everything distasteful. [...] Tramp life to the boy is a promise of all that he wishes. It promises him change of scenery and variety of experience. In it he can see prospects of wealth and fame and, best of all, it is an invitation to be off to gain a background of adventure (*Ivi*: 292).

This last aspect was systematically charted out in Anderson's analysis, who outlined the contours of meaning in the lives of young hobos. Concurrently, he revisited the concept of adventure in a similar manner to Jane Addams (1909), but reconsidering it in the light of Park's work and Simmel's (1911) reflections. This allowed to identify one of the possible interpretation lenses through which to observe and pinpoint the profound differences of the social worlds that were being examined one by one by the young researchers.

Based on their examinations, the modern city was partitioned into natural areas, each "typified by a physical individuality and the characteristic attitudes, sentiments, and interests of the people segregated within it" (Zorbaugh, 1925: 224). These areas were huddled together in an awkward, yet tight overlap between physical proximity and social distance. Case in point the Chicago Near North Side studied by Harvey W. Zorbaugh (1929[2]: 5–6): an area in transition, wherein "all the phenomena characteristic of the city are clearly segregated and appear in exaggerated form".

In just a few square miles, one would go from the glamour of the most exclusive residential neighbourhood of the city to the squalor of the slums. In this transition the multiplicity of social typologies populating the city could be spotted: the climbers enrolled in the *Social Register* living in the Gold Coast; the "white collars" living in the world of furnished rooms: lonely and restless subjects, endlessly frustrated in their wishes; the students of the Bohemian neighbourhood, an area densely populated by women; the heterogenous underworld that during the night would move around the commercialised vice district: a meeting point for prostitutes and beggars, as well as young boys and girls dancing to jazz music; the above-mentioned hobos; the sons of Italian immigrants in Little Sicily, one of the most criminality-ridden areas of the city; and finally, the slum, the area of "human derelicts" where different customs, traditions and beliefs co-existed, intersected and overlapped.

Precisely based on the lives of these young people, Zorbaugh has affirmed: "the last vestiges of the community are disappearing" (*Ivi*: 225). This contributed to producing a context in which, at home, at school and in the streets, young people's experiences were faced with – in terms that clearly echo William I. Thomas' legacy – contrasting *definition(s) of the situation*, so that "their wishes [were] often unsatisfied" and "life organisations disintegrate[d]" (*Ivi*: 24).

This opened a rift that most of those young people bridged by giving life to an autonomous lifeworld, such as the gang, that in that context found – as the work of Frederic M. Thrasher demonstrated ($1927^2$) – its very own "natural habitat". Among the research studies conducted in Chicago, *The Gang. A Study of 1313 Gangs in Chicago* is, most probably, the one that best exemplifies the approach of the Chicago School (Short, 1963), to the point that it is generally considered "a classic of sociological exploration" (Bennett, 1981: 160) and a foundational text for *gang studies* (Monti, 1993; Knox, 1991[5]; Brotherton & Gude, 2021). Following the typical model of the School, Thrasher used a diverse methodological toolkit comprising: interviews with gang boys; census data; observation; documents and school records; data gathered by correctional and social agencies, as well as other professionals working with youth (Young, 1931). He supplemented this with specific attention to the visual dimension: in fact, the book features numerous photographs, the representation of the gangland in Burgess' chart showing the development of the city (Park, Burgess & McKenzie, 1925[3]) and a detailed map detailing the distribution of gang activities throughout the urban area of Chicago.

According to Thrasher's definition ($1927^2$: 57), the gang is:

> an interstitial group originally formed spontaneously and then integrated through conflict. It is characterized by the following types of behavior: meeting face to face, milling, movement through space as a unit, conflict, and planning. The result of this collective behavior is the development of tradition, unreflective internal structure, esprit de corps, solidarity, morale, group awareness, and attachment to a local territory.

These lines summarise the main findings of the analysis conducted among the 1313 gangs identified in Chicago. The most innovative aspect of Thrasher's work is the interstitial character of a form of organisation blending three points of view (Bennett, 1981): first of all, in line with the approach of human ecology, Thrasher noted that gangs tended to seize control of the cracks and crevices of the urban structure (the river bank, the railroad tracks or abandoned buildings, the alleys, the slums). In other words, youth gangs took hold of the city "borderlands" – areas where social control is weakened – thus opening up space for ambiguity and anomie (Thrasher, 1926). Secondly, the interstitial dimension of the gangland was apparent in that it crossed a mosaic of urban *underworlds* with shifting populations, high levels of mobility, significant levels of poverty and in general, remarkable social disorganisation. Finally, the same interstitial dimension concerned the biographies of its members. In fact, as highlighted in the following excerpt by Thrasher (1927[2]: 36), the gang:

> occupies a period in the life of a boy between childhood, when he is usually incorporated in a family structure, and marriage, when he is re-incorporated into a family and other orderly relations of work, religion and pleasure.

This insight persuaded Thrasher to enact a strategic field choice leading him to focus primarily on a wide range of youth groups – from the informal playgroups to criminal gangs (Feixa, 1998[3]; Knox, 1991[5]) – made up of youth between 11 and 25 years of age. Hence, Thrasher devoted more attention to the social groups that were more turbulent and socially visible (Park, Burgess & McKenzie, 1925[3]), yet concurrently provided a prompt and satisfactory response to the needs that the family, the school and the recreational agencies were unable to satisfy (Thrasher, 1926). In line with this analytical decision, in the second part of the book he focuses primarily on the romantic dimension of the gang, analysing its relationship with issues such as mobility, adventure, play, literature and cinema (Brake, 1985). He thus emphasised the relevance that the dimensions of fantasy and imagination – namely those set of attitudes and practices that, as will be elucidated in the next paragraph, not unlike Thomas, the author described as "the quest for new experience"– acquired in the lives of teenagers and young people.

Similarly, taking as key reference the definition of *primary group* (Cooley, 1909), in the third part of the book, Thrasher examined the forms of organisation and control that existed within the gang, delving deeper into questions of informal education, solidarity, gang jargons and coded languages, composition and – as Park termed it – the agonising quest for thrill and adventure (Park, Burgess & McKenzie, 1925[3]). The outcome is an ethnographic synthesis where "sociology itself [becomes] a form of lively, imagistic storytelling" (Polan, 2007: 306) and preserves – according to the views of Norman Denzin (quoted in Dimitriadis, 2006: 337) – the allure of a " 'filmic' text".

In hindsight, what appears to be less persuasive is the assessment of those variables such as gender, age, socio-economic status, that subsequent research has shown to be essential to the study of the phenomenon of criminal gangs (Short, 1963; Bennett, 1981; Brotherton & Gude, 2021). At the same time, a host of critics have underlined how Thrasher failed – despite the richness of his analysis – to thematically and persuasively articulate matters related to gangs' relationship with organised crime and with the political machine, on the one hand, and the ways to address the root causes of ganging and solve the issues ensuing from it, on the other (Geis & Dodge, 2000; Knox, 1991[5]; Kontos, Brotherton &

Barrios, 2003). In this sense, not unlike that of his colleagues, Thrasher's work is marred by an inherent tension between a social researcher perspective and, driven by the School's reformist tendencies, that of the "activist, a person committed to putting what he learned into practice so that the lives of others might be improved" (Monti, 1993: 17).

Regardless, the work sheds light on an aspect that stands out, to date, as incredibly thought-provoking. Norman Denzin describes it as follows:

> Thrasher insisted that gangs can only be understood in terms of their relations to other social institutions, including the family, the media, church, school, the police, the YMCA, the local park and playground. Youth and their gangs must be studied, he argued, in their situational contexts, in the performative pedagogical spaces of culture where young men and women with agency and intentionality take up their own lives and give them meaning in dramatic performances of ritual and sacred significance (quoted in Dimitriadis, 2006: 338).

Thrasher's unit of analysis was not the single gang, nor the individual (Getis, 1998). Rather, he focused on the so called "situation complex", the matrix of social, spatial and institutional factors which, in their reciprocal interlinking, conditioned and determined the activities, the movement, the experiences, behaviours and relatedly the "natural history" of the gang. As Dimitriadis (2006: 351) has noted, this was a relevant and current suggestion, to the extent that it allowed Thrasher, throughout his work, to observe and acknowledge "young men as actors in their own lives, making decisions that made sense in the context of their quotidian experiences".

## 1.3. Mapping juvenile delinquency

The theme of juvenile delinquency underpinned much of the exploration carried out by the researchers of the Chicago School. Nevertheless, it found a more advanced expression in the work conducted, outside academia, but in close collaboration with the Sociology Department, by the *Institute of Juvenile Research* (henceforth *IJR*).

The Institute was born in 1909 as *Juvenile Psychopathic Institute*, thanks to the contribution of Ethel S. Dummer. In the framework of the activities put forward by the *Juvenile Protective Association*, the Institute was asked to act as child study and guidance clinic, examining the cases of young people held in *Chicago Detention Home* and helping juvenile court judges to decide, on a case-by-case basis, the best outcome for individuals who appeared before them (Bennett, 1981). William Healy, a psychologist with a medical background was invited to lead the institute.

Aided by Augusta Bronner, Healy kickstarted a range of research studies that eventually led him to take a distance from Lombroso's theories and ideas around mental defectiveness, preferring to emphasise the multiplicity of causes conducive to juvenile delinquency: not merely those of psychological nature, but also those tied to context and life conditions (Getis, 1998, 2000). In addition, Healy (1915) underlined the need for a detailed study of *The Individual delinquent*, hinging on the administration of medical, psychological and mental tests, the collection of information from the family, neighbours, the police force and especially – and herein lies one of his most innovative contributions – from the individual's "own story". Healy (1922) did not maintain, however, that it was possible to generalise the results of one's examinations. Despite the acknowledged impact of social and environmental forces, the root cause of delinquency and more generally of all young people's behaviours could be traced back, in his view, to the emotions and in the inner mental space of the youngsters summoned to appear before the Juvenile Courts (Sutherland & Cressey, 1955).

In 1917 Healy left Chicago and the Institute was incorporated into the *Department of Public Welfare* of the State of Illinois. The name of the Institute changed and the psychiatrist Herman Adler was nominated as director. For a long time, the new *IJR* took on a clinical role, supporting the Juvenile Courts. The turning point was nine years later, when thanks to funding from *Behavior Research Fund,* an independent internal Department of Sociology, tasked with conducting long-term and longitudinal research on juvenile delinquency, was created (Getis, 2000).

Burgess, who provided ongoing guidance to the *IJR*, recommended that the management of the department be handed over to Clifford R. Shaw, supported the following year by Henry D. McKay. This was the dawn of a new era, that lasted approximately 30 years. This phase led to studying "the incidence of delinquency and crime in relation to different social and cultural backgrounds" (Shaw & McKay, 1942[2]: 5) along three axes, each aligned with a specific aspect of Burgess' thinking (1916, 1923, 1930): the mapping of the geographical distribution of delinquency; the collection of autobiographies of juvenile delinquents; the definition, as early as 1932, of a delinquency prevention programme coordinated in collaboration with social agencies.

The first area of the program developed by the *IJR* entailed a process by which the residences of delinquents, the percentages of school truancy and the official statistics on adult offenders were plotted on maps of Chicago (Shaw et al., 1929; Shaw & McKay, 1942[2]). For each period under examination, researchers took note of the location and prevalence of cases in registered city areas based on the data gathered by the courts and the police (Knox, 1991[5]). This was then used to estimate variations in delinquency rates along the major radial axes of the city centre, as well as in concentric zones drawn – following Burgess' model – from the city centre (Snodgrass, 1976).

The research highlighted that the highest rates of juvenile delinquency were attributable to specific parts of the city, particularly the so-called "transitional zone", an interstitial area sandwiched between the industrial and residential areas. Moreover, Shaw and his collaborators (Shaw et al., 1929) noted that delinquency rates declined as the distance from the city centre toward the periphery increased. The longitudinal analysis allowed to ascertain that in each of the examined areas the levels of youth delinquency tended to stabilise regardless of those "invasion" processes affecting the composition of the local population. Finally, a substantial homogeneity between data on youth delinquency, school truancy and adult crime was evinced (Sutherland & Cressey, 1955). In line with the studies conducted in other cities, these factors led Shaw and McKay (1942[2]: 315) to argue for the existence of "a direct relationship between conditions existing in local communities of American cities and differential rates of delinquents and criminals". The high rates of youth delinquency, therefore, had to be understood as an indicator of a broader social, economic and cultural disorganisation of local communities living in transition areas. This is the beating heart of their theory, namely the notion that *"deviant characteristics are a property of the environment and not of a given group or individuals"* (Melossi, 2008: 114, *emphasis in the original*).

According to Shaw and McKay, like any other cultural pattern, delinquency is socially transmitted through young people's daily interactions (Bennett, 1981; Getis, 1998). To test this notion and to further the knowledge garnered, Shaw and McKay combined statistical analysis with the collection and analysis of young delinquents' life histories: emblematic examples can be found in the autobiographies of Stanley the jack-roller (Shaw, 1930[2]) and Sidney Blotzman the "moron" (Shaw, 1931[2]), as well as in the book dedicated to the Martin brothers (Shaw, 1938).

It is worth noting that despite these works stemming from an intensive collaboration, as Snodgrass (1976: 2–3) aptly points out, there existed a clear subdivision of academic tasks between McKay and Shaw:

> McKay was quite the statistician, a man who stayed removed at the Institute and plotted the maps, calculated the rates, ran the correlations and described the findings which located empirically and depicted cartographically the distribution of crime and delinquency in Chicago. Shaw, on the other hand, was an activist, who 'related' to delinquents and got their life stories, and an organiser who attempted to create a community reform movement. McKay was the professional scholar and gentleman – polite, kind,

thoughtful – an academic out to prove his position with empirical evidence. Shaw was the emotional practitioner, a professional administrator and organiser – talkative, friendly, personable, persuasive, energetic and quixotic – out to make his case through action and participation.

Shaw was well aware that autobiography presented a host of pitfalls related to its authenticity and reliability, as well as interpretative challenges (Blackman, 2022). Nevertheless, inspired by the work of Thomas, he was convinced that, supported by supplementary materials useful "to evaluate and interpret more accurately the personal document", the latter could become a precious tool to unpack "the factors contributing to delinquent conduct" (Shaw, 1930$^2$: 1, 2). The detailed study of a case allowed, in other words, to recognise the viewpoint of young people, examine the social and cultural world they inhabited, rebuild the sequence of experiences that made up their criminal careers and thus, identify the causes of juvenile delinquency, as well as the potential strategies for treatment (Blackman, 2022). Commenting on the first case study published by Shaw, Burgess noted:

> His career is a series of acts in response to changing social situations; the discrimination of his stepmother against him in favor of her children; the freedom and release of exploration in a disorganized immigrant area; the patterns of stealing presented by the neighborhood tradition; the lures of West Madison Street; the repression of treatment in the correctional and reformatory institution; the fellowship and code of an oppressed group and the education in crime freely offered to him by associates in these institutions; the thrill of adventures in crime; the easy money quickly obtained and spent; the dullness and monotony of the chances to reform offered him. These are factors common to the actual experiences of thousands of youthful bandits and gangsters (in Shaw, 1930$^2$: 189–190).

Once again, the use of personal documents allowed to fully demonstrate that:

> A delinquent act is part of a dynamic life-process, and it is artificial to view it except as an integral part of that process. Until the delinquency is viewed in relation to its context in the life-history of the individual, it is not intelligible. Until it is made intelligible it cannot be effectively treated (Shaw, 1931$^2$: 8).

In line with the purposes of the *IJR*, Shaw (1930$^2$: 164 *ff.*, 1938: 340 *ff.*) eventually turned his focus to "treatment" in the cases he examined. In relation to this, a first hypothesis concerned outlining individual (re)education projects, centred on the reintegration of young delinquents into a new family, work and community context.

A second and more ambitious activity was the launch, in 1932, of the *Chicago Area Project* (Melossi, 2008; Blackman, 2022). As already argued, Shaw and

McKay attributed the causes of juvenile delinquency to social disorganisation. The life histories collected showed that "what was necessary was to 'restore', 'repair', or indeed 'reorganise' social relationships in a given area to the end of preventing crime" (Melossi, 2008: 115). Against this backdrop and in the light of the insights emerging from the mapping exercise delineating the phenomenon, three neighbourhoods of Chicago were identified to roll out the project. Among the residents of each area, a few "natural leaders" were selected, to whom two main tasks were assigned: on the one hand, to create local committees able to fuel a process of transformation of the neighbourhood's life; on the other, to enter in a direct relationship – given their shared belonging to a similar life context – with juvenile delinquents (Sutherland & Cressey, 1955). The aspiration was of re-activating communication and exchange channels that were typical of the community level, namely of the dimension in which Shaw and McKay had flourished (Snodgrass, 1976).

It is at this point that the intrinsic ambivalence of the *IJR*'s approach becomes apparent. Scrupulous attention toward the local community allowed Shaw and his collaborators to observe in more detail societal processes – and particularly the dynamics of juvenile delinquency – as they unfolded. Nevertheless, not unlike the pathways of many other Chicago researchers, the role played by wider historical, social and economic processes affecting the city was generally overshadowed by the micro dimension. This consideration applies both to the ecological and the life histories model (Bennett, 1981; Getis, 1998).

## 1.4. Young women

This review would be incomplete without mention of William I. Thomas, given his lifelong attention to the situation of women (Cersosimo, 2019) and young women in particular.

This specific interest comes through powerfully in *The Polish Peasant in Europe and America*, the study he co-authored with Florian Znaniecki (1918/1920) that contributed to the long-standing recognition he still enjoys (Rauty, 2020). Against the backdrop of a broader reflection on the disorganisation of the immigrant, in the fifth volume, Thomas focused on the causes of immigrant girls' "sexual immorality". The analysis of the Juvenile Court's records allowed Thomas and Znaniecki to notice how, under the circumstances faced by girls in the "new world", their sexual behaviour wasn't merely symptomatic of "generally unorganized life". Whether it should be considered as "an end in itself [...], or a means to other ends [...], or both", girls' sexual immorality seemed – in fact – to produce more profound effects than those detected among boys, which led them from being "merely a-moral" to being "distinctly anti-moral"; (Thomas & Znaniecki, 1918/1920, vol. 5: 320, 336). Even if, sooner or later, a young woman would "be forcibly 'reformed' and settled" Thomas firmly concluded that "before her dreams are dispelled she tries to realize them as far as she can" (*Ivi*: 339).

Thomas developed these matters further in *The unadjusted girl*[1]. The book, published in 1923, presented the results of a research study – supported by Ethel S. Dummer – on the behaviour of girls, with specific attention being placed on their sexual conducts and prostitution. Moving away from most of the analyses circulating at that time, *The unadjusted girl* aimed to develop a broad understanding of the "social demoralisation" of girls. Following the approach already embraced in *The Polish Peasant*, Thomas was mainly interested in analysing changes in sexual behaviour and attitudes in the light of their being "culturally conditioned" and "culturally defined", as Burgess fittingly pointed out (Salerno, 2007). At the same time, the book aimed to suggest solutions to a situation that appeared to be increasingly common (Getis, 2000).

Thomas grounded his analysis in his theory of the (four) wishes. He posited that in an effort to define the situation, the subject would listen to the wishes for *new experience*, for *security*, for *response* and for *recognition*. This constituted the starting point to make sense of the variety of expressions of behaviour. He was conscientious of the eternally unstable balance, which was couched in the unavoidable conflict between one's own aspirations and the "definitions within the family, by playmates, in the school, […] in the community" (Thomas, 1923: 43). In particular, he emphasised how in the passage from the community to the metropolitan dimension, the integrity of normative and moral codes went missing, leaving room for an inescapable process of behavioural individualisation (Salerno, 2007). This resulted in a twofold effect: on the one hand, it loosened the grip of traditional institutions on the regulation of young men and women's wishes; on the other, because of the endless tension between the acceptance and refusal of social norms, it promoted the rise of a constantly new definition of the situation, that was the premise for a permanent openness to social and cultural change.

Thomas adopted his typical research method, based on the collection and analysis of personal documents: autobiographies, records from the Juvenile Courts and other social agencies, research reports, and above all, letters, such as

---

1   It is worth noting that in April 1918, after having been accused of breaching the *Mann Act*, Thomas was arrested and fired from the University of Chicago. He moved to New York, where he worked as a freelance researcher (Bulmer, 1984).

those sent to newspapers like *Forward*. Almost evoking the words used in *The Polish Peasant*, the analysis of these documents brought him to acknowledge that:

> The beginning of delinquency in girls is usually an impulse to get amusement, adventure, pretty clothes, favorable notice, distinction, freedom in the larger world which presents so many allurements and comparisons. The cases which I have examined (about three thousand) show that sexual passion does not play an important role, for the girls have usually become 'wild' before the development of sexual desire (Thomas, 1923: 109).

With the weakening of traditional codes and their coercive hold, the definition of the situation of girls was influenced by what was seen in shop windows, in fashion, billboards, cinema and romance magazines. While it was possible to distinguish between those who had occasional sexual encounters and those that were publicly recognised as prostitutes, Thomas concluded with a few lines that evoke Bertha Thompson's subsequent autobiography (Reitman, 1937), and thereby sum up the crux of his research: "Their sex is used as a condition of the realisation of other wishes. *It is their capital*" (Thomas, 1923: 109, *emphasis added*).

Ultimately, *The unadjusted girl* offers plentiful materials through which one can observe, in their most intimate and personal unfolding, the aspirations and desires of the girls whose stories are retraced. Related to this, a key element is apparent and can be considered as his "theorem" as expressed in the closing of *The Child in America*: "if men define the situation as real, they are real in their consequences" (Thomas & Thomas, 1928[2]: 572). The way this is articulated in *The unadjusted girl*, shows that this dynamic does not refer to the single act, but to the ways in which the very personality of those girls was moulded, as well as to the differences that time and again emerged between different individuals and groups. To this end, despite the criticisms raised against their use in Thomas's work (Blumer, 1939[3]: 117 *ff.*), personal documents allow to grasp the different forms of human behaviour in the incessant interweaving between normal and a-normal, compliant, deviant and "unadjusted" (Salerno, 2007).

The theory of the (four) wishes is a fundamental contribution that we shall focus on – a mainstay being the study conducted by Paul G. Cressey as part of his dissertation, defended in 1929, and published as *The Taxi-Dance Hall* (Cressey, 1932a[2]). Cressey examined the demoralisation process of young women in the context of the transformations that invested leisure in the urban dimension. In particular, the research sought to offer a detailed representation of the distinct characteristics of the social world of *taxi-dance halls*, the social backgrounds and life-cycle of the taxi-dancers, proprietors and patrons, and the natural history of the institution, as well as of those ecological conditions that favoured its spread, and the social control mechanisms operating within it.

In the four years spent on the research, Cressey's collaborators carried out a complex process of ethnographic observation, striving "to become as much a part of this social world as ethically possible" and "to keep as accurate a record as possible of the behavior and conversations of those met in the establishments"[2] (*Ivi*: xviii).

The *taxi-dance halls* were spaces with "unsavory reputations" (Salerno, 2007: 121), generally situated in contexts of extreme mobility, where clients could dance with young people paying the equivalent of a taxi ride: one *dime* (10 cents) for each dance, lasting approximately one and a half minutes. This was a context in which the relentless individual searched for new stimuli, and the development of commercialised recreation and a growing promiscuity, inextricably and mutually intersected.

Several aspects of Cressey's analysis stand out. First, anticipating many of the features that are attributed to youth subcultures, he underscored how that of the *taxi-dance hall* was a distinct social world, "with its own ways of acting, talking, and thinking. It [had] its own vocabulary, its own activities and interests, its own conception of what is significant in life, and [...] its own scheme of life" (Cressey, 1932a[2]: 31). Moreover, he stressed how, with the only exception being security, in this special social world all the wishes identified by Thomas found full satisfaction (Salerno, 2007). More generally, within the so-called "sex-game", typical dating models were subverted: on the one hand, the dancer considered her clients as "means" useful to achieving her goals; on the other, the patron was "interested in securing an attractive young woman with whom he may dance and converse without the formality of an intro-duction and without many of the responsibilities entailed at other social gatherings" (Cressey, 1932a[2]: 40).

In these spaces, heterogeneous interests and subjects would meet. A diverse mix of clients found in the *taxi-dance hall* a space that welcomed them as equals and offered them the "first opportunity for social contacts with American young women" (*Ivi*: 153). Then there were the dancers: very young girls, often foreign,

---

2   It is worth recalling here the distinction between two possible roles of the observer that stand side by side with the possibility of identifying one's intimate friends as a source of research data: the "*sociological stranger*" and the observer who mixes as an "anonymous" equal or stranger (Cressey, 1983), the latter adopted in the exploration of the *taxi-dance hall*: a choice that has sparked many methodological and ethical questions (Bulmer, 1983; Dubin, 1983; Salerno, 2007).

who had severed their ties with the communities of origin and were moved by "a type of emancipation in their sexuality", able to reconcile financial wellbeing with the satisfaction of their desires (Salerno, 2007: 123). For both these individuals, entering the *taxi-dance hall* constituted the beginning of a process of "personal demoralization". In particular, as Cressey put it, once they entered this social world, the girls commenced a career based on a series of "retrogressive cycles": when their status inside a group dwindled, they moved on to a new group (or a new room) of progressively lower status in ethnic, social or physical terms, acquiring once again, albeit only temporarily, a – relatively – prominent position. The lowliest option, for those who failed to embrace other life trajectories, was prostitution, a lingering presence in *taxi-dance halls*, as well as in the public debate surrounding their creation and the *social reform* proposals around their existence in the urban dimension (Gelder, 2007).

Nevertheless, while they might have in fact contributed to enhancing demoralisation, according to Cressey *taxi-dance halls* also responded to a mishmash of desires that remained unfulfilled in the multi-ethnic metropolis. It follows that "the problem of the taxi-dance hall can be regarded as the problem of the modern city" (Cressey, 1932a[2]: 287). Taxi-dance halls can be understood – once again – as a symbolic microcosm of that rapidly changing society (Salerno, 2007): the impersonality, the weakening of controls, the loneliness and the maladaptation distinctive of the urban reality can, in this way, be immediately revealed. This offers the opportunity to understand the (ambivalent) life trajectories and cultural patterns of young women and men who live in it (Rauty, 1995[3]).

## 1.5. Motion pictures and youth

In their detailed account of the event, Jowett, Jarvie and Fuller (1996), describe how in July 1928 Reverend William H. Short travelled to Chicago to recruit scholars hailing from different departments to join the team entrusted with the implementation of an ambitious project on *Motion pictures and youth*. Developed in the context of the *National Committee for the Study of Social Values in Motion Pictures* (rebranded in 1931 as *Motion Picture Research Council*), the project sought to collect scientific evidence on the influence of movies on children and youth – instrumental in endorsing a censorship campaign. Short had received funding from the *Payne Study and Experiment Fund* (hence the trademark *Payne Fund Studies* – hereafter *PFS* – by which these research studies are generally known) and could rely on the robust support of public opinion (Grieveson, 2008).

In the face of the growing relevance of the film industry in the recreational activities of young people, there was a widespread and growing concern about the potentially negative repercussions that the world represented in the *"house of dreams"* (Addams, 1909) could have on younger audiences (Chicago Motion Picture Commission, 1920; Mitchell, 1929). Moreover, potential links between the growth and spread of the cinema industry and juvenile delinquency were also being intimated (Polan, 2007; Malin, 2009).

In the working group coordinated by Werrett W. Charters, a group of researchers originated from the University of Chicago was included: Frank N. Freeman from the School of Education; Louis L. Thurstone and Ruth C. Peterson from the Psychology Department; Robert E. Park and Herbert Blumer from the Sociology and Anthropology Department, who were later joined, as we will see shortly, by Frederic M. Thrasher and Paul G. Cressey.

Questions related to the media, popular cultural and communication processes had traditionally piqued the curiosity of the Chicago School. Hence, Park was very pleased to receive Short's invitation (Grieveson, 2008) and was undoubtedly drawn towards this brand of work, in view of his journalism background. As Buxton (2008: 348) argues, they had a lot in common: consistently with Short's hypotheses, Park was persuaded that "the values to which children were exposed in dime novels and movies […] were at odds with those that were being taught in the central institutions of civil society" and could therefore reveal themselves as "antisocial values". With the help of young Herbert Blumer, Park suggested the development of two studies – *"1000 cases of delinquency"* and *"Youth conduct and the movie"* – aiming to analyse the data on juvenile delinquency gathered by the Juvenile Courts and social agencies, and compare the effects of movies on the behaviour and attitudes of young middle-class students and juvenile delinquents. In 1929, Park was awarded a fellowship to visit China and Japan and was forced to abandon the project. The responsibility for the relationship with Short and Charters fell entirely on the juniormost member of the team (Grieveson, 2008).

Initially, Blumer turned his attention to the collection of autobiographical testimonies from over 1500 students attending university, college or high school. The analysis of the texts produced by the students allowed him to delve deeper into their personal experiences, thus highlighting "the different kinds of ways in which motion pictures touch the lives of young people" (Blumer, 1933: 8). Based on this, in *Movies and conduct* Blumer "explored" the influence of cinema on play, dreams and fantasy, the emulation by adolescents of the beautification, dress, mannerisms and love techniques of Hollywood stars, the forms of emotional possession that lay at the heart of watching movies, and more generally, the ability of movies to offer young people schemes of life that could shape their attitudes and behaviours. He thus concluded that due to the failure of educational institutions to provide adolescents with the adequate knowledge to step into the world of adulthood,

> motion pictures organize his needs and suggest lines of conduct useful for their satisfaction [...;] define his role, elicit and direct his impulses, and provide substance for his emotions and ideas (*Ivi*: 195, 197).

These findings were corroborated by a second research study, *Movies, Delinquency and Crime*, conducted in collaboration with Philip M. Hauser and dedicated to the investigation of the influence of cinema on delinquency and crime. Blumer and Hauser (1933) adopted tools that had already been tested among middle-class students (namely, interviews, life histories, brief essays and questionnaires), which in this case were administered to a sample of juvenile delinquents, inmates and former convicts, as well as boys living in a high-rate delinquency area. They complemented all this with a questionnaire for the directors of penal and correctional institutions. Based on the data gathered, the two researchers argued that the film industry could contribute to juvenile delinquency in two ways. Directly, by offering intel on crime techniques that young people could mimic, or encouraging confidence towards delinquent activity, whether as a one-off act, or as part of a criminal career (Buxton, 2008). Indirectly, "by reason of subtle and often unconscious effects, may unwittingly dispose or lead individuals to various forms of misconduct", whilst also potentially fuelling an attitude of greater tolerance toward juvenile delinquency, bringing to light issues related to social control (Blumer & Hauser, 1933: 198).

Blumer's work constitutes – a theoretical and methodological – contribution of great value for the subsequent development of studies on mass communication. At the same time, his perspective is extremely guarded. He recognised, at least partially, the role played by deterrence in some movie plots and emphasised the need to pay attention to the content of each production and of the background of each spectator (Jowett, Jarvie & Fuller, 1996). However, displaying a consonance of approach – that was never really dissimulated – with the mastermind behind *PFS*, in both studies the sociologist privileged cinema's "suggestible, [...] mimetic and deleterious" effects (Grieveson, 2008: 21):

> the forte of motion pictures is in their emotional effect. [...] As we have sought to show, [...] impulses and feelings are aroused, and the individual develops a readiness to certain forms of action which are foreign in some degree to his ordinary conduct (Blumer, 1933: 198).

As Buxton (2008: 348) rightly pointed out, "Not surprisingly, in line with the assumptions of his mentor Robert Park, he concluded that Hollywood films provided standards for youth that could potentially have a harmful effect on their conduct".

Notwithstanding his contentment with Blumer's work, Short was still "impatient for very clear evidence of causality [...] between delinquency, crime and the movies" (Jowett, Jarvie & Fuller, 1996: 71). To strengthen the unit dedicated to the investigation of this relationship, on Park's suggestion, in 1929 Short roped into the project Frederic M. Thrasher, who in the meantime had transferred to New York University. The author of *The Gang* suggested to frame the analysis in the context of an ongoing project – the *Boys' Club Study* – geared towards assessing the educational and prevention efficacy of recreational programs offered by the *Boys' Club* in areas of New York, densely populated by migrants (Polan, 2007; Merico, 2015).

After the team spent two years working on a survey considered by Short and Charters unsatisfactory and ultimately sterile, Thrasher nominated Paul G. Cressey[3] as head of the unit on the *Boys' Club Study* focusing on cinema. The researcher of *The Taxi-Dance Hall* entirely re-designed the methodological set-up of the research, combining questionnaires with over 20 other data-gathering techniques, ranging from interviews to participant observation and life histories (Cressey, 1932b). Moreover, Cressey and Thrasher emphasised the need to study film consumption with reference to the "total situation" (Thrasher, 1928) in which the daily life and the education of young people from Intervale, pseudonym for the area of New York examined in the research (Anderson, 2008), unrolled.

The richness of this new material captured the attention of Short, who saw a window of opportunity to enrich the analytical framework of *Motion picture and youth*. However, at the end of the first year of research, the sociologist had a so-called *"intellectual epiphany"* (Jowett, Jarvie & Fuller, 1996: 86). In fact, Cressey (1938: 518) stressed the methodological misconception undergirding

---

3   Cressey's incorporation in the team was foreshadowed by a heated discussion among the promoters of *PFS*. In fact, his engagement had been tainted by an accusation for sexual assault in connection with his research on *taxi-dance halls*. There was a widespread suspicion that while he would paint his role of researcher as that of an *"anonymous stranger"*, as Charters phrased it, the harsh reality was that there was "something wrong with him sexually" (quoted in Jowett, Jarvie & Fuller, 1996: 85). Nonetheless, precisely this study had helped *PFS* professionals to take a glimpse into "an unconventionally skillful researcher of disorganized social milieus" (Anderson, 2008: 51).

the assumption "that accurate knowledge of the cinema's 'contribution' can be deduced from particularistic studies of the motion picture experience". Rather, in his view, it was necessary to expand the object of analysis, taking into consideration wider interrelations between the big screen and the subject, and the latter and their social world (Buxton, 2008). This intuition allowed Cressey (1934; 1938) and Thrasher (1936) to identify the multitude of functions carried out by cinema and movie theatres in the experiences of individuals and communities. They thus demonstrated that "movies should not be linked to boys' delinquency, but must instead be viewed as a powerful source of 'informal education' that served boys in a far more direct and practical way than did schools or the Boys' Clubs" (Jowett, Jarvie & Fuller, 1996: 86). Therefore, cinema could not be considered as a univocal and unilateral force, nor could it – as Blumer had argued – be a source of potentially harmful influences (Buxton, 2008). Rather, Cressey accentuated the active and reflective role of the spectator and the possibility of "*motion pictures*" to act as a mirror through which second generation migrants could access cultural models and lifestyles that would pave the way for their "Americanisation" (Polan, 2007; Anderson, 2008).

These notions were in conflict with the beliefs held by members of the *PFS* team who shared Charters' outlook (1933: 61), the latter being convinced that: "these impartial studies […] clearly indicate that the power [of the motion picture] flows too much in dangerous". In fact, according to the two New York University researchers, under no circumstance could film consumption be considered as a direct cause of juvenile delinquency. On the contrary, they posited:

> In a society in which there are many factors making both for disorganization and social amelioration, the cinema is an important social and educational force contributing directly and incidentally to both (Cressey, 1938: 524).

Thus, the chasm among the *PFS* gradually deepened (Anderson, 2008), alongside the frustration of many researchers vis-à-vis the cursory discussion of these issues made by Henry J. Forman in *Our movie made children* (1933), serving dissemination and propaganda purposes. More generally, there was a noticeable step away by many from what appeared to have turned into a "moralizing crusade" (Jowett, Jarvie & Fuller, 1996: 7). Between the end of 1932 and the start of 1933, overlapping personal and health problems significantly slowed down Cressey's and Thrasher's work. Despite having been announced on several occasions by Macmillan, the book *Boys, Movies and the City Streets* which would have included the findings of their research, was never completed. Unlike the remaining 13 contributions, it has remained unpublished.

## 1.6. Looking back to Chicago

The "golden era" of the Chicago School and its distinctive sociological creativity lasted until Park's retirement in the mid-1930s (Bulmer, 1984). In the meantime, most of those who contributed to the pathway described so far had left Chicago. Thomas moved to New York; Anderson relocated to Washington, New York and finally Jersey City; Thrasher and Zorbaugh were recruited by E. George Payne to work at the New York University's Department of Educational Sociology in 1927; Cressey followed suit in 1931; in 1931 Blumer replaced Mead as lecturer in *Advanced Social Psychology*; and in 1932 Shaw and McKay launched the *Chicago Area Project*.

The analysis articulated in these pages cannot, in any way, fully exhaust the vast array of research conducted by the Chicago School on the experiences of young people. We have selected the most relevant pieces to underscore the most prominent characteristics of the journey along which researchers attempted to identify and give voice to the different profiles of young people who lived in and left their mark on American cities in the 1920s.

Undoubtedly, the sociological eye of "the men of the Chicago School" (Deegan, 1988[2]) was biased, in that it did not give the complexity of the reality it examined, its due recognition. It ended up turning the spotlight only on certain social typologies or areas of the city (Rauty, 1995[3]). Thus, the gaze focused primarily on those young people – almost exclusively young men – who were marginalised or struggled to integrate and thus populated the interstices or the most socially disorganised areas of the urban reality. The risk of a reading that tangibly connects the experiences of young people with deviance and delinquency (Berzano & Genova, 2015) and that relies, as is the case in many of those research studies, on a "pathologizing discourse" (Dimitriadis, 2008: 32), eschewing a systematic reflection on the relationship between young people, organised crime and mafia, should not be underestimated (Knox, 1991[5]; Reynolds, 1995). Concurrently, some have also pointed to absence of a reflection on questions of conflict, power and social stratification, as well as the lack of an explicit critique of social organisation, evident in the work – including that on youth subcultures – of Chicago researchers (Brake, 1985). Moreover, the collaboration with social and philanthropic entities hints to an unresolved ambivalence between the definition of an exploratory process and the engagement of researchers in a reform process that was affecting the United States at that specific historical juncture (Getis, 1998). Finally, in the works of (young) researchers of the School one can detect, on the one hand, a form of *appreciation* (understanding or sympathy) towards the subjects and social worlds studied (Matza, 1969); on the other, as Greg Dimiatridis

(2006: 335) has pointed out, a "naïve sense of excitement, of discovery", the most evident consequence of which is the presence in their contributions of frequent normative positions.

Without underplaying these aspects, it is however essential to highlight the pivotal nature of their works, able to successfully bridge "the gap between [...] theory and empirical research" (Bulmer, 1984: 224) and impact in significant ways the future development of the sociological analysis of youth and youth cultures. These are not research studies systematically or specifically orientated towards the analysis of youth cultures (Hebdige, 1988[2]). However, the works stemming from the Chicago tradition are generally perceived to be "the first comprehensive study of 'urban youth' " (Dimitriadis, 2008: 27). Over time they have inspired fruitful theoretical perspectives and important research experiences (Gelder & Thornton, 1997; Campbell, 2000[2]). One can find references to this in the research of Elmtown of Hollingshead (1949), Albert K. Cohen (1955), William F. Whyte (1943[2]), Howard Becker (1963) and the researchers of the Second Chicago School, as well as in the studies on urban subcultures by the *Centre for Contemporary Cultural Studies* of the University di Birmingham (Berzano & Genova, 2015).

In fact, in these works it is possible to make out the theoretical and methodological concepts that continue to inspire, in different ways, contemporary research on youth cultures. The following is a non-exhaustive list: the importance given to the use of personal documents and the attempt of combining ethnographic, ecological and statistical analysis (Bennett, 1981); the attention devoted to the *urban* root causes of many cultural youth manifestations and practices (Dimitriadis, 2008); the recognition of the complexity and internal differentiations of the cultural system of youth groups (Berzano & Genova, 2015); the ability of researchers to come to terms with the complex articulation of a kaleidoscope of social types of young people in the urban landscape.

In any case, one must give Chicago researchers their due for having married in their work the ability to analyse sensitive issues such as marginalisation, deviance, criminality, social control and any other type of so-called *social problem* with broader themes and dimensions of the day-to-day life of young people, such as free time, educational processes, lifestyles, symbolism, the relationship with the media and so on. These issues have struggled to gain salience in other, much more recent, analytical attempts towards understanding youth cultures.

## 2 Youth and generations. Background, contents and (in)actuality of Karl Mannheim's perspective

### 2.1. An outdated concept?

David I. Kertzer (1982: 28) has asserted that "few key terms of sociological discourse have been so consistently muddled in their definition and application as that of 'generation' ". Since August Comte, the humanities and social sciences have associated radically different meanings and interpretation models to the notion of "generation". Despite being an intrinsically polysemous concept (Bengtson, Furlong & Laufer, 1974; Kertzer, 1983; Pilcher, 1994), that of "generation" represents a widely employed – and oftentimes abused – tool in research on young people (Woodman, 2016).

In contemporary social thought, the concept of generation, Feixa and Leccardi (2010) argue, has received particular attention at three historical junctures: between the two World Wars, when the philosophical foundations of coexistence and generational succession, and the notion of "generational relay" were explored; in the 1970s, the season of youth and student protest, with a specific focus on matters related to the "generation gap" and generational conflict (which we will return to in Chapter 4); and after a long phase of neglect, from the second half of the 1990s, alongside the rise of the network society, the concept started gaining renewed traction to interpret the privileged relationship between young people and technology-based innovation processes.

Despite their specific articulations, these trajectories share an essential commonality: the concept of generation offers an analytical perspective of particular importance to the study of social and cultural transformation processes. In other words, in light of their ability to (re)produce, time and again, constantly novel competing styles of life and thought, generations can be understood as one of the main agents of social change (Laufer & Bengston, 1974). Young people play an essential role in the process of change, as they are responsible for continually instigating transformation.

This argument has been explored in detail in Karl Mannheim's theoretical framework, which continues to represent a mainstay of sociological research on young people and youth cultures (Furlong, Woodman & Wyn, 2011; Wyn & Woodman, 2014; Woodman, 2016). Undoubtedly, as he himself underscored, just like any theoretical perspective, Mannheim's analysis must be understood against its historical and intellectual backdrop, and ought to be approached critically. In our view, this is a much-needed exercise to (re)calibrate the heuristic value of a concept that for manifold reasons could appear *outdated*. Nonetheless, if understood in its broader articulation – that, as we will see, goes beyond the definition of the concept of generation – the perspective offers analytical tools that are instrumental, to this day, to unpack contemporary social phenomena.

In the following pages, we will outline the theoretical background and the main contents of Mannheim's analysis of the "Problem of generations"; in the central part of this Chapter we will focus on the insights developed by the Hungarian sociologist on the theme of social change and the role of young people; in conclusion, linking back to several key highlights of his theory, we will strive to prove the contested (in)actuality of Karl Mannheim's contribution to youth cultural studies. At the heart of the journey embedded in these pages is the firm conviction that, although Mannheim forged a path that is rich in contradictions, his reflections leave room for a multiplicity of readings, able to prompt new reflections, analytical perspectives, key themes and research questions, that are extremely current and relevant to any scholar studying generations and young people.

## 2.2. The sociological "problem of generations"

Originally published in 1928 in the journal *"Kölner Vierteljahrshefte für Soziologie"*, "The problem of generations" was initially unappreciated, largely because it was considered a rather negligible publication in the broader landscape of Karl Mannheim's scientific production. Upon invitation of Julia Mannheim, wife and long-standing collaborator of the sociologist, in 1952 Paul Kecskemeti included it in the collection *Essays on the Sociology of Knowledge*. This allowed for its broader dissemination – thanks to its translation into English in particular – and enabled a reconsideration of the interpretive potential of the Hungarian sociologist's theory. In fact, starting with the outbursts of student protest in the 1960s and even more clearly afterwards, the essay has asserted itself as a cornerstone of the study of generations and their relationship with processes of change (Edmunds & Turner, 2002; Feixa & Leccardi, 2010; Woodman & Wyn, 2014; Woodman, 2016; Popescu, 2019).

The essay published in the collection edited by Kecskemeti coincided with the consolidation of the very same theoretical frame in which it had originally been elaborated, namely as an application of the method of the *Sociology of knowledge* (Kecskemeti, 1952; Pilcher, 1994; Edmunds & Turner, 2002). The essay, appears, in fact to seamlessly correspond with the outline traced by Mannheim during the years he spent in Germany: as he argues in *Ideology and Utopia*, the objective of this sub-discipline is that of studying the development of thought in relation to the social and historical structures it is rooted in, with the objective of analysing the existential, cultural and social conditions of knowledge. At the heart of this reflection is the re-elaboration of Marxist theory, leading Mannheim to distinguish between what he calls a "particular" and a "total" conception of ideology. However, the core of his conceptualisation revolves around the concept of "social determination of knowledge", one of the most contradictory and critiqued aspects of the Hungarian sociologist's theory (Coser, 1971; Mayo, 1990). With the clear objective of giving continuity to the path set by Marx ed Engels in *The German Ideology*, by re-reading the work in the light of the lessons learned from German historicism, Mannheim emphasises that thought and knowledge cannot be understood merely as individual activities, nor as the result of forces that eschew the experience of the social group. Rather, each form of knowledge is the result of a historically and socially situated process and is always re-elaborated based on the specific position occupied by individuals in society. Furthermore, Mannheim intends to demonstrate that beyond class, there are other social categories able to condition the production and re-production of knowledge: "status, groups, sects, occupational groups, schools" and as far as we are concerned here, "also generations" (Mannheim, 1929: 276).

Based on the analytical model typical of his work, in the first part of the essay, Mannheim outlines the main contributions made by different theoretical and disciplinary approaches to the study of generations, focusing his attention on positivism and the "romantic-historical" approach in particular.

Embracing a unilinear conception of progress, positivism viewed the succession of generations as the analytical node needed to begin comprehending the direction of social change (Pilcher, 1994). August Comte, the main thinker associated with this approach, argues for a direct link between the rhythm of progress and the succession of generations, measured in quantitative terms: "the pace of the former could be calculated simply by measuring the average time required for one generation to be replaced [...] by a new one" (Feixa & Leccardi, 2010: 9). Progress is thus understood as resulting from the balancing out of conservative forces linked to older generations and the reformation potential expressed by new generations. Enthused by the aspiration to find a general law of historical development, the objective of positivists is thus that of identifying the average duration of intervals within which a new generation replaces the previous. However, in this way – Mannheim (1952: 278) stresses – they end up excessively crediting a perspective that is rooted in continuity, where social time, generation succession and progress itself "are thus directly attributed to biological factors".

According to the main advocates of the second approach examined herein, the generational dynamic can be evaluated only through a qualitative and spiritual approach. The main reference in this case is Wilhelm Dilthey. For the German philosopher – emphasises Mannheim (*Ivi*: 281) – "the problem of generations is seen [...] as the problem of the existence of an interior time that cannot be measured but only experienced in purely qualitative terms". Generations do not follow each other according to a predetermined pace: rather, "what matters most is the quality of the bonds that hold a generation's components together" (Feixa & Leccardi, 2010: 9). In turn, these bonds are rooted in the intersection of intellectual and social influences. Accordingly, as argued by the art historian Wilhelm Pinder (1926), generations come into being when a new "entelechy" affirms itself, as expression of the unity of the "inner aim" of a new generation, namely "its inborn way of experiencing life and the world" (Mannheim, 1952: 283). In conclusion, rather than the succession of generations, what truly interests scholars embracing the "romantic-historical" approach, is the sharing of *experiences* able to shape a common sense of being and the emergence of a shared identity (Abrams, 1982).

Of the two theoretical standpoints analysed, Mannheim underscores the specific inclinations, the shared elements and those he rejects, with the aim of articulating his understanding of the "problem of generations" rooted in a sociological perspective able "to work out the simplest, but at the same time the most fundamental facts". In particular, with an eye to distinguishing biological phenomena from those deriving from social and cultural factors, Mannheim appropriates the method of "Formal Sociology" (Simmel, 1950; Tenbruck, 1965), as a means to identify and categorise the different pathways of generation succession. This allows him to open up to a dynamic perspective and to be attuned to the historical phenomena that he is studying.

Despite the ongoing attempt to integrate his approach with other emerging perspectives, Mannheim is indebted to German historicism, which irrevocably influences his analysis of the concept of "generation". Employing a different reading of the interpretation put forward by Wilhelm Dilthey, he points out a first key argument of his reasoning:

> The same dominant influences deriving from the prevailing intellectual, social, and political circumstances are experienced by contemporary individuals, both in their early, formative, and in their later years. *They are contemporaries, they constitute one generation, just because they are subject to common influences* (Mannheim, 1952: 282, *emphasis added*).

He does not hesitate, however, to bring the analysis back to an exquisitely sociological level. In fact, the contemporaneity to which he refers is not merely chronological: it becomes relevant only as it expresses a specific "social location" (*lagerung*) – a concept borrowed from Marxism, which he uses in a broader sense. Not unlike class position, the concept of generation does not depend on a single person's voluntary commitment and is independent of whether the person has or doesn't have consciousness. The generation *location* (*Generationslagerung*) is produced by belonging to a collectivity of individuals, born in the same time frame, the same social and historical space, and via the possibility "to experience the same events and data, etc., and especially that these experiences impinge upon a similarly 'stratified' consciousness" (*Ivi*: 297).

The most pressing problem Mannheim faces is to emphasise how the generational *location* represents one of the sociological variables underlying the existential determination of knowledge (Pilcher, 1994). In fact, in line with a process that can be associated to that affecting social class, each specific generational *location* sets the boundaries of "a specific range of potential experience": it narrows down, in other words, the horizons available to individuals who are part of it, constraining certain modes of thought, experience, and action. At the same time, the *location* stemming from belonging to a generation produces a positive effect, as "a tendency pointing towards certain definite modes of behaviour, feeling, and thought" (Mannheim, 1952: 291), that the sociologist can recognise and circumscribe precisely in light of that belonging.

If, on the one hand, generations allow to identify and study the pathway along which cultural processes are historically situated, in Mannheim's perspective, they represent above all, a social factor able to favour the development of new styles of thought and understandings of the world (Feixa & Leccardi, 2010; Woodman, 2016). To this end, the sociologist repeatedly insists on the fact that the positioning of generations is a *potentiality*, that in the historical process can come into being, be suppressed or be embedded in other social forces.

To clarify the ways through which generational discontinuity emerges and the reasons that make it indeed possible, Mannheim introduces the distinction between generation *location*, generation as an *actuality* and generation *units*. Differently from generational *location*, the notion of generation as *actuality* (*Generationszusammenhang*) does not represent the mere contemporary display of the same experiences: rather, it signifies what Edmunds and Turner (2002: 8) have defined as an "active category", because it expresses the connection that comes into being as a result of the "*participation in the common destiny*" of a historical and social unit that is able to produce a concrete bond between members of a generation. This *actuality* brings individuals together, as, even if in different ways, "they participate in the characteristic social and intellectual currents of their society and period" (Mannheim, 1952: 303–304): in other words, it creates a reciprocal bond between those who consciously and actively engage with the social/historical destiny of their era.

Within every generation as an *actuality* different generation *units* (*Generationseinheit*) can emerge. While representing a much more defined reference point than the concepts of generation *location* and generation as an *actuality*, according to Mannheim, generation *units* are not akin to a "concrete group", based on its members' mutual acquaintance or created for specific objectives. Rather, a generation *unit* is defined in the light of two elements: firstly, the consciousness of its individual members, characterised by a broad affinity of contents and experiences; secondly, its "formative tendencies" (deriving, for instance, from "the profound emotional significance of a slogan, of an expressive gesture, or of a work of art"), where the social relevance lies in their "power to bind individuals socially together". Thus, a "socializing effect" – as Mannheim calls it – unfolds, joining together disparate objects in space and thereby guaranteeing spatial and temporal continuity to the principles which the generational link rests upon (*Ivi*: 305). Therefore, signalling a second key aspect of his reflection, the generation *units*:

> do not merely involve a loose participation by a number of individuals in a pattern of events shared by all alike though interpreted by the different individuals differently, but an identity of responses, a certain affinity in the way in which all move with and are formed by their common experiences (*Ivi*: 306).

The application of the "Formal Sociology" method thus allows Mannheim to underscore the process along which, against the backdrop of subsequent elaborations, the potentiality inherent in the generation *location* and shared in the generation as an *actuality* translates into a concrete force for social and cultural change, precisely when the generation *units* take form. Let's delve deeper into the mechanics of this process.

## 2.3. Generations and social change

According to Mannheim, while representing an essential premise, biological factors (being born, growing up, aging) aren't sufficient to develop a sociological analysis of generations. Such analysis can only be carried out by paying specific attention to the social and historical processes within which generations are born and follow each other (Pilcher, 1994). As Abrams put it (1982: 240), "the problem of generations [...] is a problem of the mutual phasing of two different calendars: the calendar of the life-cycle of the individual and the calendar of historical experience".

Based on this, questioning the ways in which subsequent generations can become aware of their unity, Mannheim (1952: 309) observes that "it appears probable that the frequency of such realizations is closely connected with the tempo of social change". He seeks to underscore that not all generations develop their own identity, able to make a break with the past. In the static (or slowly changing) communities, where change follows a cumulative process rooted in tradition, one does not witness the progressive differentiation between – eternally new – generation *units*, as the socialisation of new members takes place within a culture that is already deeply entrenched. Change, while taking place, is gradual rather than brisk and radical, and thus is not conducive to a stark break with the past (Mitterauer, 1986). On the contrary, in dynamic societies – where social change takes place at a more intense pace, cultural heritage needs to be constantly renovated – it is up to the younger generation to renew outdated cultural models.

While drawing on different premises and theoretical standpoints, here Mannheim's analysis overlaps with that of José Ortega y Gasset as articulated in the cycle of lectures held in 1921–1922 (Fields, 1994; Feixa & Leccardi, 2010; Caballero & Baigorri, 2019), now gathered in *The modern theme*. Arguing that each generation is torn between two choices – either to accept and appropriate the experience of the previous generation or swim with the tide embracing its own spontaneity – the Spanish philosopher has underscored the Janus-faced nature of the historical giving and receiving of generations:

> There have been generations which felt that there was a perfect similarity between their inheritance and their own private possessions. The consequence, then, is that ages of accumulation arise. Other times have felt a profound dissimilarity between the two factors, and then there ensue ages of elimination and dispute, generations in conflict. In the former case the young men coming to the front coalesce with the old and submit to them: in politics, in science and in the arts the ancient regime continues. Such periods belong to the old. In the latter case, since there is no attempt at preservation and accumulation, but on the contrary a movement towards relegation and substitution, the old are swept away by youth. Such periods belong to the young and are years of innovation and creative struggle (Ortega y Gasset, 1923: 17–18).

In the second case, the cultural heritage assets which have been accumulated (and transmitted) by the previous generation "have been deprived of their lustre, of their attractive power and of their authority" (*Ivi*: 79). The new generation does not recognise the "sacred" nature of tradition, as the latter is unable to act as a reference in the new context. On the contrary, Ortega y Gasset posits that the new generation is imbued with an unadulterated "vital sensitivity" (different from previous and subsequent generations) that defines its "historical mission" (Feixa & Leccardi, 2010). For this reason – as exemplified, albeit in a distinct manner, by Ortega y Gasset and Mannheim – in the periods when change is more sweeping, young generations, given the lack of a deep-seated cultural heritage, perceive their identity as aligned with the ongoing transformation which is taking place. They absorb key elements of innovation thereby contributing to the rise of new approaches, lifestyles, values and shared cultural models (Bodei, 2014).

To go back to the *formal* perspective suggested by Mannheim, it is within this process that generation *units* can carve out the distinctive features of their cultural heritage and (re)create their own collective consciousness, separate from that of previous generations (Berger, 1960; Cavalli, 2004). It is thus possible to summarise these reflections by stating that:

> New styles of identity can be made only within the specific historically constructed possibilities of the world entered by any given biological generation. If a new sociological generation is to emerge, a new configuration of social action, the attempt of individuals to construct identity must coincide with major and palpable historical experiences in relation to which new meanings can be assembled (Abrams, 1982: 255).

In relation to these elements, it is important to underscore that Mannheim does not go into excessive details about how the potentialities intrinsic to a generation *location* contribute to the rise of a new generation as an *actuality* and relatedly, to new generation *units*, and thus to the production and reproduction of change (Mauger, 1990; Woodman, 2016). In his essay on generations, the sociologist does not seem, in fact, to explicitly tackle the issue of identifying the direction and conditions wherein the potentialities of a generation can turn into reality (Edmunds & Turner, 2005): rather, he repeatedly insists on the role played by the social and cultural structure and more specifically, by the impact and rhythm of social change (Cavalli, 2004). It is thus impossible to determine which events might affect it. In the final part of the essay, Mannheim (1952: 312 *ff.*) reflects on the relationship between generational phenomena and "other formative factors in history", attempting to identify the cultural and social *milieu*, which is most conducive to novel entelechies (new relationships and generation *units*). However, he does not achieve the depth of the analysis reached in the definition of the concept and "forms" of generation succession. For instance, when he identifies in "intellectuals" – and more generally, in groups that can advance new styles of thinking in view of their external and marginal positioning – one of the main forces able to activate a process of transformation, he does not clarify how the ideas "generated" by these individuals can gain traction and popularity in the broader social context. He almost appears to legitimate a partial reading of the complex intersections undergirding generational dynamics, which stands in contrast with the more innovative aspects of his theoretical proposition (Chisholm, 2002).

It is important to recall that, precisely due to its biological roots, generation succession is understood by Mannheim as a continuous process, leading to a systematic "fresh contact" with cultural heritage. This "fresh contact" coincides with the emergence of a new generation producing, in his view, considerably more radical effects than those generated "by mere social change" affecting an individual: in fact, in the first case, subjects "who are in the literal sense beginning a 'new life' ", who lend scarce importance to the heritage passed on to them by their ancestors, are concerned (Mannheim, 1952: 293). Thus, the generational dynamic finds its rationale in the sheer questioning of the inventory of cultural assets:

> The continuous emergence of new human beings certainly [...] makes a fresh selection possible when it becomes necessary; it facilitates re-evaluation of our inventory and teaches us both to forget that which is no longer useful and to covet that which has yet to be won (*Ivi*: 294).

Without generational change, the cultural heritage of a group would remain trapped in past experience and memory (Cavalli, 2020). It would lack that decisive thrust towards transformation that can be otherwise seen in the social element, which represents the synthesis between the biological and historical dimensions. Accordingly, "the transmission of a common cultural heritage is always reflexive, interactive and precarious" (Edmunds & Turner, 2002: 8).

These considerations allow to grasp the decisive role that Mannheim ascribes, in his reflection on generations, to young people in processes of transformation. Here, once again, Mannheim's reflection overlaps with that of José Ortega y Gasset. As Feixa and Leccardi (2010: 15) point out, the Spanish philosopher has developed a sort of "paradigm of the regenerating force of the young people" based on which the latter were "replacing the proletariat as emergent subject and the generational succession was replacing the class struggle as an engine for change". In Mannheim's perspective, youth represents the moment in life when individuals develop the ability to interrogate themselves independently and come to grips with their social and historical positioning. According to Mannheim (1952: 297–298), the role played by "first impressions" is essential. They represent individuals' "*natural view* of the world", the starting point from which to define the relationship with future experiences, that won't simply add up, but will be orientated and interpreted *dialectically* in relation to the previous, giving rise time and again to a new " 'stratification' of experience".

The sociological relevance of youth is manifest in the fact that, in this phase of life, the individual experiences with greater intensity the symbolic power of the *present*:

> The 'up-to-dateness' of youth therefore consists in their being closer to the 'present' problems [...], and in the fact that they are dramatically aware of a process of de-stabilization and take sides in it. All this while, the older generation cling to the re-orientation that had been the drama of their youth (*Ivi*: 300–301).

To this, we must add a second factor, equally meaningful in Mannheim's reasoning, namely the dearth of *experience* which characterises youth:

> That [...] youth lacks experience means a lightening of the ballast for the young; it facilitates their living on in a changing world. One is old primarily in so far as [...] he comes to live within a specific, individually acquired, framework of useable past experience, so that every new experience has its form and its place largely marked out for it in advance. In youth, on the other hand, where life is new, formative forces are just coming into being, and basic attitudes in the process of development can take advantage of the moulding power of new situations (*Ivi*: 296).

Herein emerges a theme, that is dear to Walter Benjamin and, more generally, to the romantic movement of the early 1900s (Caygill, 1998). In 1913, in one of his earlier works on the *Metaphysics of Youth*, the German philosopher and sociologist had argued that a full appreciation of youth can only take place if one lifts "the mask of the adult". For Benjamin, that "expressionless, impenetrable, and ever the same" mask is the equivalent of "experience". By acting as spokesperson for a generation fighting to take on new responsibilities, Benjamin posits that adults devalue "the years we will live, making them into a time of sweet youthful pranks, of childish rapture, before the long sobriety of serious life". Nevertheless, he claims, there is another way to understand "experience" as "most beautiful, most untouchable, most immediate". It is only by rejecting the instinct toward conservation that shields itself behind an adult's experience, that can one aspire, he asserts, "to anything great or new or forward-looking" (Benjamin, 1996[5]: 3, 5).

According to Mannheim, this means that the impact produced by sociocultural transformation takes on different connotations and meanings based on the specific phase of an individual's life. In particular, during youth, the symbolic power of "new impulses" ends up tacitly questioning both the influence of the agencies of socialisation and more generally, of memory and of adults, making it possible (and necessary) to re-define the main cultural models. When this takes place within a social/historical space that is radically different from that of previous generations, namely when young people are "exposed to the social and intellectual symptoms of a process of dynamic de-stabilization" (Mannheim, 1952: 303), the *potentiality* which is implicit in a generational *location* can crystallise itself and transform into a tangible force for change (Cavalli, 2004). It can thus engender the phenomenon of generation as an *actuality* and give rise to new generation *units*.

The ideas and ways of thinking advocated by young people who share the "formative tendencies" of each *unit* thus contribute to the creation of cognitive maps able to influence, like never before, the actions of the individuals who draw on them (Cavalli, 1994). The cultural models of these *units* are destined to become deep-rooted and long-lasting, as well as substantially autonomous from those who actually suggested them. These models become an appealing and binding force, at least until the next disruption or historical hiatus, which, when the time comes, will call for a novel stratification of experiences, thus re-activating the generational dynamic and turning back the spotlight on young people and their ability to reach harmony with transformation processes.

It is apparent that the reflection on the theme of generations (and more specifically, the attention given to young people within processes of change) allows to grasp the tight interrelation – somewhat echoing the concept of generation as "a dynamic compromise between mass and individual" (Ortega y Gasset, 1923: 15) – which Mannheim identifies between the interactions of individuals, groups, social structures and the passing of time (Woodman, 2015, 2016). The premises that allow to untangle the relationship between identity and the issue of generations, against the backdrop of a "society [which] must be understood as a process constructed historically by individuals who are constructed historically by society" (Abrams, 1982: 226), become clear.

## 2.4. Youth as outsiders

In "The problem of generations" Mannheim addresses a theme that was previously uncontemplated in his work. In his subsequent scientific production he will often use it as exemplification of the themes gradually addressed, yet will no longer treat it systematically (Chisholm, 2002). The generations-change link thus becomes the common denominator of different periods of his biographical and intellectual experience – the Hungarian, the German and finally, the British one (Wolff, 1971; Loader, 1985; Woldring, 1986).

On the one hand, the essay on generations is so affective, that in instances, it appears to eschew the scientific rigour that is typical of Mannheim's work, thus testifying to a cultural climate – common in European culture since the turn of the 19th Century – that entrusted to an "autonomous youth culture" the mission "to act as an agent of a general cultural renewal" (McCole, 1993: 35). This leads to hypothesise his own personal involvement, as if the theories articulated in the essay had somehow sparked from "a period of extraordinary social and intellectual ferment", namely from the symbolic strength and thrust toward change that had characterised his upbringing (Kecskemeti, 1952: 2).

The connection with the subsequent phase is perhaps even more manifest. During his stay in England, where he sought refuge in 1933 following the rise of Nazism, Mannheim comes to grips with the need to take stock of the broader "crisis" affecting European democracies (Mannheim, 1935), to make a *Diagnosis of our time* (Mannheim, 1943). The desire to identify a "third way" that is not conflictual, and able to prevent both the risks of a totalitarianism and the disintegration of the value system of laissez-faire, translates into his suggestion for "democratic planning", tasked with solving the tensions between substantial and functional rationality and bureaucratic control and freedom.

Within this reflection, in "The Problem of Youth in Modern Society"[1] Mannheim goes back to the sociological connection between generational dynamics and transformation processes. Mannheim's novel analysis is animated by two questions:

> What is the meaning of Youth in society? What can Youth contribute to the life of society? (*Ivi*: 31).

At the heart of the work lies the hypothesis that the *sociological function* of youth rests with being a *latent resource* "which every society has at its disposal and on the mobilization of which its vitality depends" (*Ivi*: 32). Youth is thus intended as a *"revitalizing agent"*, able to actively contribute to social transformation and favour the "adjustment to quickly changing or completely new circumstances" (*Ivi*: 34). This distinct characteristic should not be attributed, according to Mannheim, to a young person's unique propensity towards specific political ideologies or currents of thought. It does not depend on conditions of biological nature, nor on youth's greater spirit of adventure. Rather, the determining aspect

---

1   Mannheim first presented the paper at the *New Education Fellowship Conference* (Oxford, April 1941), followed by a lecture given to the *Masaryk Society* (Oxford, May 1941), and finally at the *Youth Leaders' Conference* organised by the Board of Education (Oxford, July 1941). The essay was then included by Mannheim in *Diagnosis of our time* (1943), a book bringing together the conference proceedings and speeches given in the early 1940s in England, predominantly in non-academic settings.

is the fact that young people have not accepted the social order as a given. Differently from adults, who maintain a clear grasp on their habits and customs, which inhibits their ability for openness and adaptation to novelty, youth achieve "the conflicts of our modern society from without. And it is this fact which makes youth the predestined pioneer of any change in society" (*Ivi*: 35).

Mannheim identifies in a young person the typical *outsider*:

> In the language of sociology being young mostly means being a marginal man, in many respects an outsider. [...] In my view, this outsider position is a more important factor than biological fermentation in making for changeability and openness, and it tends to coincide with the outsider attitudes of other groups and individuals who for other reasons live on the fringe of society [...]. Of course, this outsider situation is a potentiality only and [...] it depends very largely on the management and guiding influences coming from outside whether this potentiality will be suppressed or will be mobilized and integrated into a movement (*Ivi*: 36).

The distinction between static and dynamic societies takes on a new explanatory potential. In fact, while the former are primarily based on the experience of the elders and struggle to elicit the potentialities expressed by young people, the latter hinge on cooperation with and among youth, channelling vital resources into turning around the tendencies of social development.

Unlike what he had maintained in "The problem of generations" and possibly influenced by the events that struck Europe at that point in time, during the conferences held in the early 1940s, Mannheim embraces a less disillusioned and in instances activist perspective, that seems to echo Walter Benjamin when – in a 1914 publication on "The Religious Position of the New Youth" – he states: "Youth stands in the center, where the new comes into being" (Benjamin, 2011: 168). Yet this has to do, above all, with a point of view which does not hold back from openly critiquing institutions, and taps into the desire to identify strategies to translate into a socially active force the *potential* for change of new generations.

Specifically, he underlines that the activation of the *latent resource* expressed by younger generations, depends, in large part, on their ability to handle it, direct it and organise it. In other words, to ensure that youth innovation can express itself, it is necessary for societies to favour action and mobilisation via specific forms of integration and co-ordination. In an attempt to tease out the concrete ways through which young people could contribute to the transformation of social assets, he states, with reference to British and European society between the 1930s and 1940s:

> If youth is really to become a pioneer for the new cause, only a nation-wide policy of Youth will help us. That means that we have to set free that spontaneous fermentation

which is taking place all over the country, encourage its integration into a broad stream, and give youth a fair chance to become helpers in a comprehensive movement working at current tasks and for social reconstruction (Mannheim, 1943: 47).

Mannheim is conscious that his suggestion to extend the model of "democratic planning" to youth politics is riddled with contractions, because, as he recalls, totalitarian regimes have often found their legitimation in the symbolic relevance of youth. Fascism, Nazism, the Soviet Regime have, in fact, based their propaganda around the heroic symbolism of the warrior, of the young person perceived as bearer of the *future of society* and ambassador of ideology (Passerini, 1997). Nonetheless, Mannheim cautions about the risks of misunderstanding the symbolic and the real exhortation of youth carried out by totalitarian regimes, arguing that the resort to youth comes as a result of the dynamism of those societies and their uneasiness with social and cultural change. In light of this, looking at the challenges faced by British society in the early 1940s, he emphasises that, to come to light and not fall back on the experience of totalitarianism, the process of democratisation must be rooted in "new institutions, new men, new values" (Mannheim, 1950: xviii). In line with the analysis dating back to the years spent in England, he claims that:

> Unlike the brutal wholesale regimentation of dictatorships who allow only one cast of thought and action, equally unlike the passive abstention of laissez-faire Liberalism from taking any side at all, this militant democracy will have the courage to come out into the open for certain basic values common to all; yet it will, on the other side, leave the more complicated values to free individual choice and decision (Mannheim, 1943: 49–50).

To give consistency to this process it is nonetheless pivotal, according to Mannheim, to lend renewed and specific attention to education. In the essay on generations, he had attributed a secondary role to education in the broader scenario of issues concerning *"transmission of the cultural heritage"* (Mannheim, 1952: 299 *ff.*). In the years spent in England, he recognises its rising importance, concluding that: "the sociological approach looks at education not as an aim in itself but as a part of the social-historical dynamics" (Mannheim & Stewart, 1962: 160). Education thus becomes a pivotal moment for "social reconstruction", as it represents the tool to make young generations more aware of the actual needs of an ever-changing society, offering them the necessary resources to attend to the duties of modern society (Canta, 2006; Casavecchia, 2017).

As regards the key matters addressed here more specifically, Mannheim posits that to encourage the contribution of young generations to social reconstruction, the politics in their favour ought to be supported by a concurrent transformation of the educational system, based on a strategy able to guarantee, on the one hand, "basic conformity, cohesion, habit-making, emotional training, obedience" and on the other, the "gradual emergence of those qualities […] which make for individualization and the creation of independent personalities" (Mannheim, 1943: 52). The school represents the foundation of this process, to the extent that it is able to open up to other social and educational agencies, thereby supporting the process of internalisation of a democratic interpretation of life, stimulating and accelerating social and cultural change. Therefore, this pathway cannot evolve merely within the school, as it requires a broader *social education*, "which arises from the influence of the educative society where we are educating through using community influences" (Mannheim & Stewart, 1962: 20; Mannheim, 1950).

According to Mannheim's approach, instead of representing an obstacle to exercising freedom, if accompanied by the required interventions in the field of youth politics and education, social planning becomes a tool serving the full achievement of democracy in modern society, and allowing the *latent resource* represented by young generations to become an active force for change.

## 2.5. Critical aspects

Drawing on the etymology of the term "generation", we could argue that by questioning sociology's specific contribution, Karl Mannheim effectively *generates* an innovative approach: he re-combines theories and interpretative categories in novel and original ways, giving rise to something completely new (Chisholm, 2008). Over time, his proposal has become the "seminal theoretical treatment of generations as a sociological phenomenon" (Pilcher, 1994: 481) and a backbone for successive generations of social scientists interested in the analysis of generations and young people (Attias Donfut, 1988; Feixa & Leccardi, 2010; Woodman & Wyn, 2014).

Clearly, as with any innovation, Mannheim's approach comes with numerous contradictions and leaves unaddressed several critical issues: the overlap between the concept of generation and that of cohort (Ryder, 1965; Glenn, 1977; Cavalli, 2004; Thorpe & Inglis, 2019); the issue of translating into practical application the concepts he proposes (Kertzer, 1983; Woodman & Wyn, 2014; Kalmus & Opermann, 2019; Duffy, 2021); the ambivalence in the relationship between generation succession and socio-cultural change (Mauger, 1990; Woodman, 2016). We wish, however, to turn our attention to another criticality, that in our view sheds light on the contradictory (in)actuality of his analysis.

In line with Ortega y Gasset's analysis, Mannheim returns on multiple occasions on the distinction between static and dynamic societies, highlighting how the emergence of new generation *units*, on the one hand, and the mobilisation of the latent resource represented by young people, on the other, are the essence of their peculiarity. However, this begs a key question: how can one interpret generation succession at a time when, to make but one example, historical events become "global", age no longer appears to be a suitable variable to explain the social positioning of individuals, and the boundaries between generations appear to be ever so malleable? In other words, what happens when, as is the case in contemporary society, the rhythm of change accelerates, the number of events able to produce potential ruptures increases, while at the same time, temporal and spatial anchors substantially weaken with ever so blatant repercussions on young people in particular? (Leccardi & Ruspini, 2006; Feixa, Leccardi & Nilan, 2016). Inspired by Ortega y Gasset's theory (1923, 1933) further developed by Julián Marias (1949), we may ask: is it possible to discern today the seeds of a *decisive* generation in which social change is greater than usual?

In attempting to answer this question, let's iron out some fundamental details. The first key factor can be found in the analysis of Alessandro Cavalli, who on multiple occasions has emphasised the dwindling possibility of pinning down "crucial historical event[s]" that can instigate clear-cut generational dynamics (Cavalli, 2004: 158), thus affecting both the sphere of lifestyles and tastes, and that of values. In other words, despite their historical relevance, landmark events such as the Fall of the Berlin Wall or 9/11 do not seem to represent "discontinuities" marking in irreversible ways the biographies of (all) young people before or after (Pirni, 2014; Cavalli, 2020).

Reconciling Mannheim with Bourdieu's take on youth and social change, June Edmunds and Bryan S. Turner (2002, 2005) have otherwise stressed that 9/11 can be understood as an episode signifying the rise of a "*global generation*". Born out of collective trauma (the attack on the *Twin towers* in New York), this generation differs from those studied by Mannheim, that were typically local and specific, and embraces, thereby giving continuity to the generation of the 1970s, an authentically global and dynamic character (*active*). Despite sharing some elements with those preceding it, the generation described by Edmunds and Turner is in many ways a "new" generation. It is new, in noticeable ways, by comparison with that of its older siblings, characterised by a phase of passivity and profound apathy. It is also new with regard to that of its parents. On the one hand, it is clearly more pessimistic; on the other hand, it largely relies on online forms of global communication and mobility: it "shares its information and ideas across borders and acts with global impact" (Edmunds & Turner, 2005: 572). Nevertheless, the authors do not fail to emphasise how the immediacy and the transitory nature of media representations of global traumas ends up, in actual fact, inhibiting the growth of an active global generation able to produce longer-term effects. This aspect leads them to acknowledge that the acceleration typical of the rhythm of change set by late modernity renders the phenomenon of generations precarious and thus constantly prone to crisis.

Lynne Chisholm has put forward yet another interpretation that may help clarify this point. In fact, in her view, it is not a matter of rejecting Mannheim's standpoint; rather, it is paramount to re-consider it with greater attention, so as to recognise that "the more frenzied the pace of change, the more difficult it is to establish generational distinctiveness, because of the plethora of intermediary transitions that take place in rapid chronological succession" (Chisholm, 2008: 160). This is an element that Mannheim himself acknowledges in his essay on generations, where he cautions that "it is conceivable that too greatly accelerated a tempo might lead to mutual destruction of the embryo entelechies" (Mannheim, 1952: 310). Hence, when differences start fading, to the point of almost vanishing, the possibility of identifying new generational *locations* is not lost. Neither is the hypothesis according to which "generations are a critical component of social and cultural change" (Edmunds & Turner, 2002: ix). Rather, what diminishes is the likelihood that, at least in the short-term, "distinctive generations will crystallise out", making it more arduous to clearly identify them (Chisholm, 2008: 160). It is however important to remember, Chisholm insists, about the "potential role" – acknowledged by Mannheim and evident in his examination of British society in the 1930s and 1940s – of young people as actors able to support, against the backdrop of altered conditions and ambivalences typical of late modernity, the renewal of knowledge and practices. This provided, she argues, that there is a transition from the "what" to the "how", or to re-evoke another recurrent theme of Mannheim's, from the static to the dynamic dimension.

Accordingly, several scholars have underscored the need to devote attention both to the intergenerational and the intragenerational dimensions.

On the one hand, this means studying the relationship and the "intersections" between coexistent generations (Donati & Colozzi, 1997). As Zygmunt Bauman (2007) has aptly pointed out, the generational dynamic is not a relay, where once the baton is passed on, the previous generation stops and the new one carries on. Thus, rather than referring to a "succession" it would be more apt to talk about an "overlap" – namely a coexistence – between generations. This is a reflection that Mannheim had already made when, vis-à-vis the work of the art historian Wilhelm Pinder (1926), he had mentioned the "non-contemporaneity of the contemporaneous", namely the possibility to pinpoint multiple generations sharing the same temporal space, each with their own distinct worldview. At the same time, it is helpful to recall that each new generation does not originate in a cultural vacuum, but always has to come to terms with the notions developed by the previous generation. This has to do, in other words, with overcoming the hypothesis that a new generation can *only* see the light as a result of conflict with the one preceding it or following a chasm in cultural models, and not merely as an independent manifestation of the reflexivity of subjects (Edmunds & Turner, 2002).

However, careful consideration of the intra-generational dimension requires to dismiss the notion of "members of a generation as alike, sharing a single value or dispositional set" (Woodman, 2016: 22). Undoubtedly, this type of analysis continues to re-emerge in public debate, media representations and even in academic work. This is where the fundamental actuality of the formal perspective put forward by Mannheim resides: insisting on the articulation between generation *location*, generation as *actuality* and generation *units*, the work of the Hungarian sociologist continues to represent a mainstay of sociological studies on the phenomenon of generations, and a starting point to observe "intra-generational divisions" whether they are gender-related, rooted in social class, ethnic or linked to geographical background.

These last considerations pave the way for the critical analyses developed by Christopher Thorpe and David Inglis (2019). Interrogating themselves on the possibility of ascertaining the existence of "Global Generations" – founded on "*all* young people" sharing the same risks, chances and life situations (*Ivi*: 42) – the two scholars question the reasons why "it has become common in the recent literature on global generations to assume that Mannheim's approach *must* be outdated" (*Ivi*: 49). Four points are particularly interesting in their reflection. The first relates to the fact that many attempts to re-read and *update* Mannheim's work – such as that by Edmunds and Turner mentioned above (2002) – risk falling "into forms of determinism that Mannheim himself avoided" (Thorpe & Inglis, 2019: 43). The second links back to the confusion engendered by conflating age cohorts and generations, thus losing sight of a key pillar of Mannheim's theory. The third relates to Beck's and Beck-Gernsheim's (2009; Beck, 2008) hypothesis that Mannheim's approach is marred by "Methodological Nationalism" that is ill-suited to the contemporary dimension. Against this argument, Thorpe and Inglis (2019: 54) posit that Mannheim's analytical standpoints are "much more globally-oriented, or 'cosmopolitan', and attuned to cultural phenomena, than the critics allege". Finally, the two scholars have responded to those lamenting Mannheim's obsession with the political sphere, by demonstrating that Mannheim introduced in his analysis key elements drawing on the cultural and aesthetic spheres.

Thorpe and Inglis ease us towards our two concluding remarks. The first, previously hinted to, testifies to the dramatic difficulty – in theoretical and empirical terms – faced by those who attempt to operationalise the concept of "generation", especially in a global sense. The second, which becomes specifically relevant in the context of the discussion made in this Chapter, allows to evoke the richness of the arguments and reflection points that Mannheim's original repository of ideas can still offer today to those who seek to explore the experiences of young people and generational dynamics. This provided, the two authors caution, that Mannheim's pages are read carefully enough.

## 2.6. An open-ended debate

The reflections made in the previous paragraph show that, despite the unambiguous need to revisit the concepts and specific categories put forward by Mannheim, recently many have felt drawn towards his theory.

Apart from the views mentioned herein, it is worth highlighting the argument that "Youth and generation" is a crucial issue to study, so as to renovate the research agenda on young people (Woodman & Wyn, 2014). More generally, it is important to recall the wide debate sparked by Dan Woodman (2016: 20): according to the Australian sociologist, the concept of "social generation" "provides a framework for theorizing and researching the intersection of changing youth transitions and cultural forms with broader social transformations", allowing to overcome the epistemological and methodological rigidities, that have characterised the development of youth studies from the 1980s onwards (Chisholm, Kovacheva & Merico, 2011; Woodman & Bennett, 2015c; Woodman, 2016).

In any case, the most compelling actuality of Mannheim's theorisation on the concept of generation and on the relationship between young people and change most likely does not reside in the specific merit of the concepts developed, rather in the caution and attention that have constantly accompanied his analysis and, above all, in the endlessly open relationship he entertained with the key themes and perspectives presented.

Even if no answers are claimed, re-reading Karl Mannheim today appears to offer elements and opportunities for reflection on young people and generational phenomena that are still incredibly current. Undeniably ahead of his times, he invites readers to take stock of a youth reality where profoundly different dimensions and identities intersect. He suggests to constantly study the relationship between generations and society; he highlights the need to contextualise, from a historical, social and cultural perspective, the emergence and the succession of different "generational cultures". He urges us to recognise, on the one hand, the different effects of transformation on subsequent generations, and on the other, the contribution of young people to transformation processes. Finally, he offers an analytical perspective on intergenerational relations and the youth condition that, while not reproducible mechanically, has not lost, over time, the potential to stimulate sociological reflection and give rise to new, important questions.

Mannheim suggests a pathway that is rich in views and interpretations. He himself, however, has never felt excessively attached to any one in particular: he has approached them freely and taken on the elements that he considered to be most relevant to the definition of his overall understanding of the issues progressively examined. His pathway is one that remains, and must necessarily remain, open. For some, this is one of the clearest pitfalls of his work. Yet we are convinced that the ability to recognise and accept the inherent and intimate contradictions of social experience and sociological analysis is paramount to the study of generational dynamics, socio-cultural change and, related to the themes addressed herein, youth cultures.

# 3 Youth culture and the peer group. Looping back around to Talcott Parsons

## 3.1. The peer group and the transition to adulthood

The sociological term "youth culture" was first coined by Talcott Parsons (1942) during a speech at the 36th Annual Meeting of the *American Sociological Society*. In this occasion, Parsons went to great lengths to emphasise the role of "age and sex differences" in influencing an individual's positioning in the social structure of the United States.

Parsons' focus is on the perceived exceptional nature of the transition from childhood to adolescence in modern society, particularly within the middle and upper classes. This transition represents, according to the American sociologist's interpretation, the moment in time when an individual "first begins to develop a set of patterns and behavior phenomena which involve a highly complex combination of age grading and sex role elements" (*Ivi*: 606). If during childhood and pre-adolescence, boys and girls are socialised based on a model rooted in equal privileges and responsibilities, as they enter the adolescent phase of their lives, they are expected to interiorise novel "sex roles" (Manning & Truzzi, 1972). Parsons adds that this process entails young people's heightened engagement with behavioural models that, on the one hand, differ from those shared during childhood and, on the other, as underscored by Linton (1942), do not fully overlap with those of adults. In particular, in this first formulation, "youth culture" is viewed as manifesting a "irresponsible" orientation toward social activities: for males focusing on athletics; for females revolving around "glamour" and sexual attractiveness, the latter being, as Galland (2003: 164) puts it, "what fuels and orients all behavior in this life period". At the same time, young people's cultural models disregard the " 'serious' interests in and obligations toward curricular work" and display "a certain recalcitrance to the pressure of adult expectations and discipline" (Parsons, 1942: 606–607).

The Harvard sociologist does not mask his preoccupations in this regard. In the first place, he reprimands those adults who idealise young people's behavioural models and manifest a "certain romantic nostalgia for the time when the fundamental choices were still open", as they are guilty of "unrealistic romanticism" which is at odds with their social positioning (*Ivi*: 612, 614). Anticipating a concept that over time has gained more and more traction, Parsons holds that this idealisation is symptomatic of a brand of insecurity that affects the social roles of adults. Furthermore, it is a testament to the challenges of resolving the tensions within development processes. Nonetheless, Parsons also argues that behind young people's behaviours there may be the risk of:

> a strong tendency to develop in directions which are either on the borderline of parental approval or beyond the pale, in such matters as sex behavior, drinking and various forms of frivolous and irresponsible behavior (*Ivi*: 608).

Yet there is another, more general element to consider. As they form part of a complex structure that is separate from the remainder of society and fuels potentially deviant behaviours, the attitudes of adolescents challenge the latent pattern maintenance, both when it comes to the transmission and the internalisation of culture patterns (Parsons, 1950, 1951). The underlying fear is that the process of socialisation of young generations – which in the structural functional approach should strive towards "motivating the individual to conformity with institutionalized expectations in roles" (Parsons & Bales, 1956[2]: 156) – could turn into a "barbarian invasion" (Parsons, 1951: 208), jeopardising the order and stability of the social system.

These insights serve to contextualise the analysis of the youth condition and culture, which was articulated by structural functional sociology between the 1940s and the 1960s in collaboration with anthropologists and psychologists. The most innovative aspect of Parsons' perspective and of structural functional sociology lies in the theorisation of the relationship between the growing importance of peer groups, the rise of youth culture and young people's integration in the social system (O'Donnell, 1985; Marsland, 1993).

Adolescents and young people who *invade* the social scene from the second half of the 1940s onwards are, in fact, profoundly different from the youth who grew up during the Great Depression (Davis, 1935). As Luisa Passerini (1997: 319) persuasively argues – in the light of their numbers, their level of resources and their group consciousness – they represent "the first generation of privileged American adolescents" characterised by a striking cohesiveness and above all, "an awareness of constituting a distinct community with particular interests".

This self-awareness hinges on several typical features of the modern urban reality and on shared lifestyles that are discernible in the more and more pervasive role of the mass media (TV and radio), music (with rock and roll stars becoming popular), cinema (which ropes in young people both as protagonists and spectators), literature, and more broadly the consolidation of niche youth markets testifying to young people's importance as consumers (Miles, 2000; Wilska, 2017).

The world of youth gradually detaches itself from the family unit, and takes over high schools and colleges. In fact, around the 1950s, the United States witnessed a rise in young people's college attendance and graduation rates across genders (Jencks & Riesman, 1968[2]). The involvement in lengthier learning pathways produces a noticeable "segregation" of young people within institutions, reinforcing and legitimising their progressive separation from adults. As was pointed out by symbolic interactionism, peer groups have historically been entrusted with the definition of social nature and individuals' ideals (Cooley, 1909), as well as with the acquisition, through play, of role expectations (Mead, 1934). In the scenario painted by structural functionalism, the peer group becomes, in a very short period of time, a paradigmatic synthesis and concurrently an instigator of the transformations that affect youth culture in the United States from the 1940s onwards. At the same time, it also becomes a key focus of sociological inquiry.

Ralph Linton (1942: 590) has posited the existence of a *universal tendency* in relation to which individuals belonging to the same age group develop a category solidarity, "based upon community of knowledge and interest". According to Kinsley Davis (1935, 1940), who was Parsons' student at Harvard, this tendency becomes much more relevant, when, as was the case in the United States in the aftermath of the Second World War, the scale and breadth of change pick up the pace (Heer, 2005). In these instances, "the content which the parent acquired at the stage where the child now is, was a different content from that which the child is now acquiring": that content thus becomes rapidly obsolete and inappropriate, as it draws on values, technical and scientific competences and relational models that are no longer effectively pertinent to the social reality in question (Davis, 1940: 524). Consequently, parent-youth conflict, which is dormant when the shift is dawdling, becomes increasingly palpable in modern reality: anything and everything speaks to "the incompatibility between an urban-industrial-mobile social system and the familial type of reproductive institutions" (*Ivi*: 535), and strengthens horizontal forms of belonging and relationships, especially with reference to the peer group. The latter is perceived – according to Davis – as more competent and authoritative than parents, to offer advice and behavioural models. For this reason, it also becomes a potential factor leading to societal disintegration (Ardigò, 1966) and pervasive generational conflict (Mead, 1970).

In a book that has become a cornerstone piece for scholars specialising in youth cultures and groups, *From generation to generation*, Shmuel N. Eisenstadt re-evokes this perspective and expands on it, bridging social and historical research. The conceptualisation made by the Israeli sociologist revolves around the assumption that the existence of age groups "is not given or automatic; it occurs only under specific conditions", making them a "interlinking sphere between the family and other institutional spheres of society" (Eisenstadt, 1956: 273). Unlike particularistic societies in which "the individual is enabled to attain his full membership status within the social system through patterns of behavior acquired within the family unit", in universalistic societies "the solidarity of the social system can be effectively maintained only by patterns of behavior different from those existing within kinship units". In this last type of society, during the process of development, "at the points of transition from kinship to otherwise institutionalized roles", the individual is ushered to let go of the behavioural models absorbed within the family unit, to take on novel ones, based on "diffuse and ascriptive criteria and qualities [...] which may be common to all members of the society" (*Ivi*: 43, 50).

Another key element stands out here. As Parsons observes, during the first half of the 20th Century, the American family undergoes a profound process of change. Firstly, the nuclear family becomes increasingly socially isolated from the point of view of relationships, place of residency and livelihood. Secondly, it becomes "*a more specialized agency than before*", renouncing functions that had originally fallen within its purview, without however surrendering its role in the wider social system (Parsons & Bales, 1956: 9, *emphasis in the original*). This leads to relevant consequences in child maturation and emancipation, particularly in the mid-upper classes of society, as it paves the way for a greater and longer emotional and financial dependence on parents, particularly the mother. Outside the family unit, young people are exposed to antagonistic forces, given that modernisation and differentiation processes contribute to a general sense of expectation and give rise to a broader spectrum of choices to choose from, than in the past (Parsons, 1961a). Concurrently, new generations are encouraged to break free from their reliance on institutions such as the family or the local community, to become more markedly responsible and autonomous than was previously the case (Parsons, 1943, 1951).

It thus becomes crucial for young people to "learn, by actual participation, progressively more roles than his family of orientation can offer [them]. It is at this point that peer group and school assume paramount importance" (Parsons & Bales, 1956: 38). The extension of schooling processes (high school, college, postgraduate training) results in students gaining access to a space where the "opportunity for particularistic treatment is severely limited" (Parsons, 1959: 136) and there are different statuses to choose from. More generally, school-based socialisation allows for the progressive acquisition of competences and abilities that are required of adults, both in a *cognitive* and *moral* sense. On the other hand, the peer group enables the young person to "extend the solidarity of the kinship system to the whole social system" (Eisenstadt, 1956: 50). Interactions between peers display, in fact, typical characteristics of the primary group – such as a deep-seated solidarity among its members – and other factors typical of secondary relationships – such as the abidance by pre-determined social roles. The peer group thus represents, an in-between (or "transitory") sphere, a limbo where young people can experiment and internalise the norms and role models that undergird universalistic relationships in adult age, whilst enjoining the emotional support and solidarity of familial relations (Frith, 1984; Cohen, 1997).

For the reasons described thus far, at the intersections between family, school and peer group, young people grapple with contradictory and ambivalent pressures that exacerbate the tensions experienced at a crucial time in their development process. These elements give rise to repercussions that affect both identity-definition and positioning within the social system, and the process of carving out one's autonomy and independence (De Singly, 2000), finding a specific representation in the debate around the concept of "psychosocial moratorium".

## 3.2. The "psychosocial moratorium"

Erik H. Erikson, one of Anna Freud's students, is renowned for bringing to the table several contributions that were initially widely debated and subsequently adopted by structural functionalist sociology. Over time, Erikson's insights have become part and parcel of the *sociological lexicon*. Although his underlying objective was of "revealing the workings of an invariant process of identity-formation through socially organised sequences of interaction" (Abrams, 1982: 251), Erikson also sought to demonstrate how any given identity-type is historically produced.

According to the German-American psychoanalyst, the life cycle can be split into eight stages of psychosocial development: *Infancy, Early Childhood, Play Age, School Age, Adolescence, Young Adulthood, Adulthood, Old Age* (Erikson, 1950; 1997). Each phase is characterised by a "fundamental conflict" between the psychological needs of the individual and the needs of society, that ought to be addressed and resolved to move on to the next phase. Bearing this in mind, one can easily comprehend the importance that overcoming the "crisis" experienced during adolescence (namely identity vs. role diffusion) and later on in young adulthood (namely intimacy vs. isolation) assumes in the 1950s and 1960s in the Western world. The person who is engaged in the process of development is in fact forced into choices and decisions which will, with increasing immediacy, lead to commitments "for life". The task to be performed here by the young person and by his society is formidable (Erikson, 1968: 155).

For these reasons, those who face the transition between childhood and adulthood are granted a period of *psychosocial moratorium*:

> A moratorium is a period of delay granted to somebody who is not ready to meet an obligation or forced on somebody who should give himself time. By psychosocial moratorium, then, we mean a delay of adult commitments, and yet it is not only a delay. It is a period that is characterized by a selective permissiveness on the part of society and of provocative playfulness on the part of youth, and yet it also often leads to deep, if often transitory, commitment on the part of youth, and ends in a more or less ceremonial confirmation of commitment on the part of society (*Ivi*: 157).

The moratorium represents a varying period of time during which society offers the chance "to try out roles, relationships, identities, occupations and lifestyles" (Abrams, 1982: 253). Its duration hinges on the degree of social differentiation, the complexity of the roles that need to be assumed and the breadth of possibilities available to the individual (Côté & Levine, 1987; Côté, 2006). It follows – as Kenneth Keniston (1962) will elucidate in clearer terms – that the more complex a society and the more uncertain and tension-ridden the future faced by youth, the longer the experimentation and transition period (Cuzzocrea, 2018).

Nevertheless, it is important not to lose sight of a crucial aspect. Although socially recognised, the moratorium operates at the individual level. This means, to borrow Abrams' metaphor, "for those whose play evokes no emphatic affirmation of any particular tried self, who do not bring to the experiment a sense of direction accrued from past affirmations and denials, the passage becomes an *odyssey without destination*" (Abrams, 1982: 253, *emphasis added*).

The emergence and the consolidation of conditions of mounting hesitation, such as the ones experienced by young people at that point in time, which then spilled over onto other Western societies, can therefore be interpreted as "a great potential insecurity and the possible lack of a clear definition of personal identity" (Eisenstadt, 1962: 36). The result is a scenario where "identity crises" mould into a generalised state of uncertainty and emptiness where "young people driven into the extreme of their condition may, in the end, find a greater sense of identity in being withdrawn or in being delinquent than in anything society has to offer them" (Erikson, 1968: 254). If these are the hypotheses linking back to a "pathological" dimension, one must not forget that for Erikson the development process incessantly alternates between "fidelity" and "diversity":

diversity and fidelity [...] make each other significant and keep each other alive. Fidelity without a sense of diversity can become an obsession and a bore; diversity without a sense of fidelity, an empty relativism (Erikson, 1963: 11).

Overcoming the "identity crisis" faced in the course of one's childhood and adolescence, can only happen via the interbreeding of "fidelity" and "diversity", allowing youngsters to balance their aspirations with societal demands at that particular point in time. This balancing – concludes Erikson, via a reflection that will be echoed in the work of structural functionalist thinkers – influences their identity as adults.

## 3.3. Youth culture and social integration

These considerations link back to one of the most relevant aspects of the structural functionalist reflection on youth culture: the role played by the latter in the transition to adulthood. In his speech at the *American Sociological Society*, Parsons suggested to look into the interaction of cultural models connected with the experience of youth with the strains youngsters face in making life-changing choices:

> There is reason to believe that the youth culture has important positive functions in easing the transition from the security of childhood in the family of orientation to that of full adult in marriage and occupational status (Parsons, 1942: 614).

In his subsequent work, Parsons (1950, 1951, 1961a, 1962) repeatedly goes back to this hypothesis, detailing the reasons why, in his view, youth culture enables the transition to full adulthood. According to the Harvard sociologist, the behaviours and attitudes that make up youth culture point to a distinctively structured complex characterised by a *duality of orientation*: on the one hand, a "compulsive *independence* of and antagonism to adult expectations and authority", be they parents or teachers, is palpable; on the other, there tends to be a "compulsive *conformity* within the peer group of age mates" (Parsons, 1950: 342–343, *emphasis added*). According to him, this duality represents a potential – and in some cases, an actual – source of deviant behaviour. Nonetheless, in the structural functionalist approach, loyalty to the peer group and its cultural blueprints becomes an indispensable tool to enable the emotional maturation of the youngster and guarantee, at the same time, "the development of the disposition to perform [… the] roles" that underpin adult life (Eisenstadt, 1956: 208–209). In *The Social System* Parsons clarifies the meaning of this statement, evoking several examples of how participating in youth culture is conducive to the process of transition to adult age:

the very insistence on independence from adult control accustoms the individual to take more and more responsibility on his own. In the youth culture phase he tends to substitute dependency on his peer group for that on the parents, but gradually he becomes emancipated from even this dependency. Similarly in the relations of the sexes the youth culture offers opportunities and mechanisms for emotional maturation. The element of rebelliousness against the adult world helps to emancipate from more immature object-attachments, while certain features of the 'rating and dating' complex protect the individual during the process of this emancipation from deeper emotional involvements than he is yet able to accept. The very publicity of such relationships within the peer group serves as such a protection. Thus the youth culture is not only projective but also exposes the individual passing through it to positively adjustive influences (Parsons, 1951: 305–306).

More generally, in line with this analysis, it is possible to argue that in the interpretation already put forward by structural functionalism, youth culture is an institution marred by an inherent ambivalence: while on the one hand it expresses cultural innovation ambitions, on the other it displays the conformist traits that are necessary for social and cultural integration. In this sense, from the perspective of adults, the relationship with the cultural models of youth is defined along a continuum that alternates between the attempt to keep manifestations that are perceived as deviant in check, and a growing permissiveness.

Parsons (1962: 109) highlights that adults increasingly tend to privilege the "independence training of children" over a "type of training in strict obedience". Although this can be interpreted as growing indulgence, this shift bears witness to adults' desire to instigate high levels of self-discipline, motivation and most of all, the acquisition of greater autonomy and responsibility among young people (Parsons, 1959, 1989; Eisenstadt, 1962): crucial values to ensure a *functional* transition to adulthood in a society in rapid transformation (Galland, 2003).

In its institutionalisation, youth culture thus becomes a " 'safety valve' of the social system". The permissiveness that undergirds it allows to mitigate the intrinsic tensions and insecurities of youth, channelling them into models of behaviour, which are shared and socially legitimated in the peer group. At the same time, if considered in the light of its contribution to integration, youth culture enables a dual form of *positive* social control: on the one hand, it "keeps down the total amount of deviance" that would take over should there be an attempt "to keep youth completely in line with adult disciplines" (Parsons, 1951: 206); on the other, by offering a range of options for freedom, it ensures, even among youth, elevated motivational standards and consequently, their integration in the social system.

Ultimately, if youth culture compensates for the disavowal of the security enjoyed during childhood, the step into adulthood can happen only when the individual renounces its "seductive aspect" to take up his/her role in the social structure (Parsons, 1942: 608). In the structural functional perspective, particularly as articulated by Parsons, *loyalty* to the peer group and *conformity* to youth culture must, therefore, be considered as transitory phenomena, that in manifesting their *difference* from typically adult models, allow individuals to develop *loyalty* of purposes and *conformity* to the expectations of the social system, marking a *difference* from the cultural models shared with peers in the course of childhood.

## 3.4. An "adolescent society"?

The pathway suggested by Parsons on the topic of "youth culture" can be read against the backdrop of a more general context, where since the second half of the 1930s, in the United States, the social sciences become more and more engrossed with young people: this is evident in the mushrooming of empirical research studies aiming to garner evidence of the emergence and consolidation of adolescent and youth-based cultural models (De Maupéou-Abboud, 1966; Gottlieb, Reeves & TenHouten, 1966).

Among the various studies conducted, the largest and best documented is the one coordinated by James S. Coleman. With the intention of examining status distribution mechanisms within schools and potential strategies to make study more productive, in the spring of 1957 Coleman administered a standardised questionnaire to the students and teachers of ten high schools in Illinois, selected in view of guaranteeing a representative sample of different geographical areas and realities (from small rural towns to suburbs and large urban centres), and social backgrounds (working class youth, young people hailing from families of farmers, and upper class youth). His research strives to answer the following questions: what are the characteristics contributing to prestige? What are young people's blueprints? Which students have greater influence over others? At the heart of his reflection, there is however, a more general insight, already emphasised by Parsons: the specialisation, typical of industrial society, and the consequent and prolonged segregation of youth within schooling institutions, places youth in "a world apart", populated exclusively by peers. In particular, Coleman underscores that:

> Adolescents today are cut off, probably more than ever before, from the adult society. They are dumped into a society of their peers, whose habitats are the halls and

classrooms of their schools, the teen-age canteens, the corner drugstore, the automobile (Coleman, 1961a: 9).

Coleman notes the presence of a distinct *apartness* between generations and the emergence of an "adolescent culture"[1], with its own values and specific symbols, influenced by the mass media (the TV, the radio, the cinema) and most of all, employing its own jargon, delineating the contours of a space from which adults are excluded. Coleman emphasises three items used in support of his analysis. The first refers to loyalty vis-à-vis parents, teachers and peers: to this end, to the question: "*Which one of these things would be hardest for you to take?*" only a paltry percentage of interviewees respond "*teacher's disapproval*", while the majority are split between those – equivalent to a little over 50% of students – choosing "*parents' disapproval*" and the remainder – a little under 45% – answering "*breaking with your friend*". Coleman interprets these answers as testament to the weakening of the bond with parents and the related bolstering of horizontal solidarity. A second item used by Coleman to describe *apartness* between parents and offspring is linked to the percentage of young people who claim that they are keen to continue in their father's profession, ranging between 9,8% of interviewees from urban and suburban areas and 23% of students from rural areas. The third item is the degree of importance ascribed to "*being accepted and liked by other students*", that corresponds to the decreasing worth attributed by youth to validation by parents and teachers.

Another aspect typical of the *Adolescent society* – that has also been emphasised by Parsons, yet in the work of Coleman takes on a clearer and more relevant role – is the attention given, regardless of the internal differences based on their social status, by male youth to sport and by female youth to spending time with girlfriends, reading and listening to music (Coleman, 1961b). More generally, Coleman observes that within the social system of each school, students'

---

1  It should be noted that Coleman (1961a) occasionally uses the terms "adolescent *culture*" and "adolescent *subculture*" interchangeably, to describe the same phenomenon. Nevertheless, as Berger stresses (1963b: 396), to distinguish the concept of "subculture" "one must look not only for relatively distinctive styles of life, but styles of life which are to a great extent self-generated, autonomous, having institutional and territorial resources capable of sustaining it in crisis and insulating it from pressures from without. [...] it needs a certain durability too, a continuity over time sufficient to enable it to draw upon a stock of tradition which previous groups who have borne the subculture have left behind". For these reasons – which we will delve deeper into in Chapter 5 when looking in more detail at the concept of "subculture" – in this section we prefer to employ the first term only with reference to Coleman's work.

status is not determined by ascribed characteristics, such as for instance the social standing of the parents in the community of belonging; rather it is shaped by the behavioural models typical of adolescent culture. To this, he adds that:

> academic achievement was of less importance than other matters, such as being an athletic star among the boys, being a cheerleader or being good-looking among the girls, or other attributes (Coleman, 1960: 340).

The research thus paints a picture where little value is given to study, perceived as a form of acquiescence and conformity to the expectations of adults (Berger, 1963b), to the point that young people – girls especially – refuse to be associated with the image of the "brilliant student". On the other hand, as Bernard highlights (1961: 1), the dominant cultural models among students appear to revolve around sharing material ("certain kinds of clothes, automobiles, and the paraphernalia of sports and recreation") and immaterial possessions ("a special language [… and a] great emphasis on fun and popularity"), distributed rather homogeneously across social strata, yet assuming more importance in urban contexts.

The perception of a youth community standing *apart* from the rest of society draws attention to the responsibilities and remedies to address this profound generational *difference* (Passerini, 1997). Familiarising with the opinions and analyses of experts and social researchers, Fred and Grace Hechinger – editor of the *New York Times* expert in educational matters, and freelance writer and collaborator of the Ford Foundation respectively – give voice to the widespread worries of public opinion:

> we strongly believe […] American civilization tends to stand in such awe of its teen-age segment that it is in danger of becoming a teen-age society, with permanently teen-age standards of thought, culture and goals. As a result, American society is growing down rather than growing up (Hechinger & Hechinger, 1962[2]: x).

The main risk, they maintain, is the crystallization of a *Teen-Age Tyranny*, thereby evoking an expression adapted from an excerpt by Socrates: "Our youth now loves luxury. They have bad manners, contempt for authority, disrespect for their elders. Children nowadays are tyrants" (quoted in Hechinger & Hechinger, 1962[2]: 177). What anguishes them the most is not "the greater freedom of youth", rather "the abdication of the rights and privileges of adults for the convenience of the immature" (*Ivi*: ix). The excessive leniency of parents and teachers, the ensuing disavowal to exercise the power of control and vigilance on teenagers, alongside the importance given to self-expression free from self-discipline, have, in their view, contributed to the creation of a "tribal 'subculture' ". This has allowed young people to impose their own rules and self-determine their style of behavior, giving "the impression that the rest of society had a duty to adjust its ways and its standards to teen-culture" (*Ivi*: 23). In particular, they express their apprehension toward the role models put forward by cinema, TV, music, literature and magazines for teenagers, the prevalence of smoking and alcohol, the risks linked to driving the automobile and, above all, early dating and premature sexual intercourse, leading to a rise in the rate of teenage pregnancies.

In relation to all the above, Fred and Grace Hechinger believe it is essential to give back to adolescence and youth their role of stepping stones towards adulthood:

> For several decades now, the most insecure and most immature members of adult society have permitted, often in the name of self-expression and pseudo psychology, the most insecure and most immature adolescents to establish their own independent and sovereign culture: teen-age. The task now is to make it clearly understood that adolescence is a stage of human development, not an empire or even a colony. The mission of the adult world is to help teen-agers becomes adults by raising their standards and values to maturity rather than by lowering adulthood to their insecure immaturity (*Ivi*: 193).

Explicitly dismissing the idea that the cultural models shared by young people inevitably stem from American wealth, the urgency to curtail *Teen-Age Tyranny* calls, in their view, for a practical approach to problem-solving, rather than awaiting an extensive reform of society. To this end, their suggestion moves from the objective of regenerating the family and its values through the direct involvement of parents, urged to abandon an educational model considered too permissive, and ushered to take on an understanding attitude aiming "to establish rules and set limits for their own children" (*Ivi*: 186).

This perspective is further explored by Coleman (1961a), who strongly agrees with the argument that the "superficial" and "hedonistic" value system of teenagers is – at least indirectly – encouraged and supported by adults and that this poses a glaring problem in the face of what was perceived as an "inconsistency in their educational principles" (Passerini, 1997: 324). Nonetheless, Coleman displays scepticism toward the idea of the family re-gaining the full (and solitary) responsibility of raising children: he believes that if adults successfully bridge the divide separating them from their children, then the destinies of youth will be unavoidably intertwined with those of their families. This would detract from the project of promoting *Equality of Educational Opportunity* (Coleman et al., 1966).

The hypothesis fleshed out in the conclusion of the research conducted in the high schools of Illinois points in the opposite direction: "to take the adolescent society as given, and then use it to further the ends of adolescent education", appreciating its distinct characteristics, beginning with the ones evident in the attention given by students to athletics (Coleman, 1961a: 313). On this matter, he writes:

> Athletics has a democratizing effect, breaking up organization based on background and reconstituting it on the basis of common activity or achievement. Athletics serves an important function in motivating students. It generates strong positive identification with the school; without athletics the school would be lifeless for the student, deficient in collective goals (Coleman, 1961b: 33).

The suggestion made in the last few pages of the book is to ascertain the ways in which to successfully channel the competitiveness of *adolescent society*, with its internal criteria of reward allocation and the group hierarchies, into education. This objective can be reached, according to Coleman (1961a: 322), by organising competitions and tournaments between schools (and not between individuals) "in all activities ranging from mathematics and English through home economics and industrial arts to basketball and football", contributing in such manner to promoting creativity and allegiance with the school, as well as, more generally, to stimulating motivation and students' achievement (Coleman, 1960).

## 3.5. Youth culture and the value system

In the interpretation suggested by Parsons, youth culture absolves an important function: that of latent pattern maintenance, contributing in such a manner to preserving and transmitting the system's distinctive culture and values. This is an aspect to which the sociologist dedicates specific attention in the first few years of the 1960s within a broader reflection on the problem of social transformation, which will lead him to develop a theoretical model that will serve to study the modalities through which the system strikes its balance despite changes in the general structure (Gerhardt, 2002).

At the core of the theory lies the acknowledgment of a cybernetic hierarchy of control governing interrelations between the structural components of society: values, norms, collectivities, and roles (Hamilton, 1983). Pivotal to this theory is the process of (structural) "*differentiation*" of units (collectivities or roles), in the light of which simple structures are divided into functionally differing components, thus leaving behind functions that are recombined into differentiated units. For the system to obtain renewed balance, three processes must take place. Firstly, a re-definition of the prescription of rules, namely the re-definition of the system's normative order ("*normative upgrading*"). Secondly, both the old unit and the new one must relate to each other and be recognised as a legitimate part of the wider system ("*inclusion*"), thus building "a new collectivity structure within which both types of units perform essential functions" (Parsons, 1961b: 236). The last process is of "*value generalization*": the functions carried out by the differentiated units can be legitimated only within more general complexes of institutionalised norms, namely only if the values and relatedly, the legal norms and standards of competence, performance and achievement, are detached from their original contexts to become general cultural principles that are more abstract and universal.

As Parsons points out, the three processes which have just been outlined unroll along a longer time frame than that of the process of differentiation. This leads to several important implications, particularly accentuated by modernity, that can be contextualised with reference to the condition of youth in the 1950s. Firstly, young people are asked to act and choose against the backdrop of a normative vacuum, as the boundaries between what was legitimate and what no longer is, and between what was not legitimate and now is, are yet to be clearly defined. At the same time, young people find themselves grappling with the contradictory demands of structurally different institutions: on the one hand, those that have historically been tasked with socialisation (the family, the school, the church), still linked to a normative model that is slowly declining in legitimacy; on the other, those produced by differentiation processes (the college, university and the peer group), expression of a normative model that still hasn't gained a strong foothold. Finally, Parsons (1962: 119) highlights that, unlike previous generations, adults "cannot provide direct guidance and role models that would present the young person with a neatly structured definition of the situation", because adult agencies are somehow "out of tune" with the transformation processes that are taking place. In a nutshell, "his elders simply do not have the knowledge to guide him in".

Based on these assumptions, he maintains that "it is inevitable that our children and grandchildren cannot be brought up to follow the same paths that we did". In this regard, "the question is not whether the younger generation are different", as, precisely in view of their transformation processes, "they are and must be" (Parsons, 1961a: 286). Rather, it is important to understand if, following the change experienced by the social structure due to the acceleration of transition processes, they have abandoned or still identify with the dominant American value system (1997, 1961), that Parsons calls "instrumental activism". This value system foresees the direct involvement of the individual both in the "maximal objective understanding of the empirical conditions of action" and in "the faithful adherence to normative commitments". On the other hand, the development of society "in the direction of progressive 'improvement' […] is to be through the autonomous initiative and achievements of its units – in the last analysis, individual persons". Moreover, from a moral viewpoint, this model is expressed in an "*institutionalized individualism*" that gives prominence to "the desirability of autonomy and responsibility in the individual", the ability to contribute to building a "*good society*" and equality of opportunity (Parsons, 1962: 101–102).

In contrast with the common fears of the time among adults and the press (Passerini, 1997), Parsons states:

> My own view is that, as a group, they have not [… abandoned the central values which have given its main thread of continuity to our society]. Though understandably at certain points hesitant and uncertain, and some, as always, deviant, the youth of today seem to me to be active, eager, and ambitious for achievement. They are exerting great effort to secure training for worth-while achievement and they are certainly as concerned as any generation with the all-important standards of justice and equity. I would think it very difficult indeed to prove that any previous American generation has had higher ideals as our society has defined its ideals (Parsons, 1961a: 286).

According to Parsons, therefore, young Americans have not renounced the values that make up "instrumental activism". On the contrary, he claims to nurture "high confidence that our values are intact and viable, are being successfully transmitted to our children, and can be expected to play a major part in bringing about a future for our society of which our children or children's children can justly be proud" (*Ivi*: 287).

Why is it, that in stark contrast with the argument made in 1942, come the 1960s, Parsons is so optimistic? Ultimately, he concedes that his insistence on full adherence to the value system by young people is not based on any kind of reliable "documentation". Parsons identifies several dimensions that, despite the tensions emanating from the ongoing process of change, seem to lend credence to the hypothesis of a growing integration of young people in the social system and to their renewed commitment to American values, particularly autonomy and responsibility. The first of these dimensions pertains to learning processes and can be subsumed under the positive response given by students to educational expectations and their copious efforts to access the best colleges and universities. The second links back to the transformation of relationships within the family unit: "the newer generation of parents […] tolerates more freedom" but requires young people to display "higher levels of performance" (Parsons, 1962: 115–116). The third dimension concerns more directly the "typical" features of youth culture. Parsons maintains that in the 1950s, "a significant change […] from the somewhat frenetic atmosphere of the "flaming youth" of the 1920's and to some extent of the 1930's" has occurred, evident in particular in the declining attention given to the "cult of physical prowess", to a significant "moderation in the use of alcohol", a growing " 'seriousness' in the field of sexual relations", and a mounting fascination with the arts (music, literature, drama, and painting) (*Ivi*: 116). Finally, he notes a shift in the relationship between young people and politics:

> Recently, there seems to have been a kind of resurgence of political interest and activity. It has not, however, taken the form of any explicit, generalized, ideological commitment. Rather, it has tended to focus on specific issues in which moral problems are sharply defined (*Ivi*: 117).

Parsons interprets the disaffection of youth as an attempt to voice their desire to be *more considered* and have greater influence in political decision-making: a fact that he believes to be irreconcilable with the distribution of governmental functions in a system of large-scale organisations like the American one. Despite taking into account "elite youth's resonance to the diagnosis of the current social situation in terms of conformity and mass culture" – stigmatised as "an easy disparagement of the society" (*Ivi*: 120) – young people's renewed interest in politics and their dissatisfaction with the status quo testify, according to Parsons, a new phase of "activism". They constitute, therefore, an additional, more *effective* indicator compared to the others, of the fact that "the main orientation of youth seems to be in tune with the society in which they are learning to take their places" (*Ivi*: 118).

The analysis of the transformations influencing youth culture therefore allows Parsons to validate the hypothesis that, despite leading to a generalisation of the content component, processes of change do not effect shifts in the pattern component of the shared values model (Parsons, 1961b). It is evident here that the Harvard sociologist is not concerned with comprehending how young people contribute or could contribute to social change, but rather, is interested in teasing out the consequences that change may produce on young people's shared cultural models. This is an approach that aligns with a more general process and stops short of interrogating the genetics of the culture, limiting itself to the analysis of the interiorisation of a pre-existing reality by a single subject. At the same time, the analysis of youth culture offers a notable exemplification of the pathway along which the imbalances determined by structural differentiation are subsumed under a process of adaptation that captures any emerging tension and lures it back into the neat systemic web (Cohen, 1997). A pathway that guarantees, as Parsons stresses in the conclusion of his speech at the *Taminent Institute*, balance and stability in the face of prospective *challenges*:

> Clearly, American youth is in a ferment. On the whole, this ferment seems to accord relatively well with the sociologist's expectations. It expresses many dissatisfactions with the current state of society, some of which are fully justified, others are of a more

dubious validity. Yet the general orientation appears to be, not a basic alienation, but an eagerness to learn, to accept higher orders of responsibility, and to 'fit', not in the sense of passive conformity, but in the sense of their readiness to work within the system, rather than in basic opposition to it (Parsons, 1962: 122–123).

## 3.6. Between sociological analysis and "myth"

Taking youth culture as the object of analysis, social research appropriates itself of a topic that is particularly heartfelt by public opinion (Cartosio, 1992). As previously mentioned, the young people living in the years following the Second World War are perceived as the social category which most exemplifies the contradictory demands of the reformation process that sweeps over American society (Modell, 1989; Austin & Willard, 1998). At the heart of this transformation, there is, without a shadow of a doubt, the baby boom, which interlocks with processes of social, economic and cultural nature, revolutionising the relationship between young people and adults. To re-evoke what was already emphasised in the previous pages, the numbers of young people accessing high schools rises; the socialisation role, historically played by the family, is delegated to a heterogeneous mix of secondary institutions; the peer group takes on a leading role in the lives of new generations; a consumer industry specifically targeting teenagers takes hold; and young people start being more active in the cultural and political spheres (Kett, 2003).

In an attempt to make a contribution to the rising demand for knowledge in the social sciences, Parsons, Eisenstadt, Coleman and the other scholars mentioned in previous pages, define the contours of a new *object* – youth culture – recognising sociology's and the social sciences' prominent role in its study. The reflection stemming from American structural functionalism thus coincides with the richest and most vivacious season of sociological analysis on matters related to youth and their cultural expressions (Brake, 1985).

The analytical pathway set by Talcott Parsons has, in fact, represented and continues to represent an essential and foundational pillar for anyone conducting research in this field (Frith, 1984), having Parsons consistently anticipated some of the main themes and interpretation tools (Turner, 1999; Furlong, 2013; Wyn & Cahill, 2015). Suffice it to think of the analysis on the relevance of the peer group, the transformations within the family and in the relationship between parents and children, the growing relevance of the mass media, the role of consumption in the definition of youth's models of behaviour, or the critical aspects linked to transition to adulthood and more generally, on the extension of the youth phase (Galland, 2003; Côté, 2014).

Moreover, in line with the work conducted by the Department of Social Relations (founded in 1946 by Parsons in collaboration with Gordon Allport, Clyde Kluckhohn and Henry Murray), a large part of the reflection on youth culture developed by structural functionalism has the benefit of being rooted in an interdisciplinary approach, where the sociological perspective is in constant dialogue with the anthropological one, as well as with social psychology and psychoanalysis.

A comprehensive evaluation of the perspective on youth culture developed by Parsons and by structural functionalism, shows however that the main theorisation which is put forward appears to be *partial and unfulfilling*, in that it is unable to coherently explain the plurality of conditions that young Americans face after the Second World War (Berger, 1963a). Rather, almost anticipating what will soon after assert itself as a dominant representation, that is the "romanticised" reality of American suburbia portrayed in *Happy days*, they limit themselves to describing only a side of it: white, middle-class, primarily male students. In this manner, the scholars end up dismissing the noticeable differences between genders and ethnic groups, in the conditions faced by Black people, by youth of rural areas and children of the urban working class – which are documented in the important monographic issue of the "*Annals of the American Academy of Political and Social Science*" edited in 1961 by Jessie Bernard and devoted to the analysis of *Teen-Age Culture*.

A second aspect relates to the possibility of understanding youth culture as an institutionalised response to the tensions that emerge along the development pathway. While the hypothesis of defining adolescence as a period of "*storm and stress*" has found – starting from G. Stanley Hall's (1904) pioneering work – support in psychological and sociological research, as well as in the representations offered by rotogravure, lifestyle magazines and cinema, it is crucial to remember that this representation is typical of a specific historical and social context (Musgrove, 1964) and has taken on distinct features at different historical moments and along different social strata. This is exemplified by Margaret Mead's (1928) research in the Archipelago of Samoa and stands as evidence that specific representation cannot, therefore, be applied extensively to all young people (Elkin & Westley, 1955). At the same time, it is crucial to take into account that many young people acquire their identity as adults without these kind of experiences (Wyn & White, 1997). It is also possible to face similar experiences at different moments of one's life (Berger, 1963a).

More generally, the argument that the representation of *one* youth culture, intended as a repository of values and shared behavioural models endorsed by the near totality of the population of adolescents and young people, is a "pseudo-problem", gains traction (Elkin & Westley, 1955). In fact, the previous analysis had ended up ignoring the fact that "not all teen-agers participate in the teen-age culture": in other words, not all young people subscribe to the values, norms, preferences and styles falling under the concept of youth culture (Smith, 1976). As Bernard points out (1961: 2), those who participated in the debate, were well aware of this:

> those who are in the civilian labor force […], who are in the armed services […], or who are married […] are chronologically, but not necessarily culturally, teen-agers. They are neophytes in the adult culture of our society. They may share some aspects of teenage culture, but, for the most part, they are expected to perform adult roles in adult dress. Teen-age culture is essentially the culture of a leisure class.

Going back to his analysis of the role played by generational groups in socialisation processes through the lens of the student protests of the 1970s, Eisenstadt himself recognises the need to devote specific attention to the "diversification" of the cultural models that denote the youth groups belonging to different social contexts, starting from the assumption that "youth is not perceived as a homogeneous category, nor is it any longer necessarily the confrontational category it used to be" (Eisenstadt, 1971[3]: xxiii). Without dismissing the gaps emphasised by Eisenstadt first, and then by Parsons and Coleman, in that same period, social research turns its attention to three key aspects: (a) the existence of continuity between the cultural models that young people share, and between those of childhood or adulthood; (b) the presence of a significant number of young people who conform to the cultural models put forward by their parents (Elkin & Westley, 1957); (c) the possibility of identifying the seed of many contents typically attributed to youth culture, in adult culture.

More generally, where there is an "extension of cultural definitions of 'youth' to a period covering at least 20 years and sometimes longer" (Berger, 1960: 13), there is also a need to analyse the differences that are noticeable within the same population of youth, whilst also taking into account that chronological age and the more strictly cultural dimension (intrinsic to the adjective "*youthful*") may not be correlated. In this direction, as Bennett M. Berger (1963a: 325) provocatively suggests, it could be possible to make a dual analytical distinction: on one hand, between "youthful young men", namely those bearing characteristics considered typical of youth culture, and "unyouthful young men", who are alien to that culture; and on the other, between "unyouthful old men", who are such both biologically and culturally, and "youthful old men", those who despite biologically adult, adopt the cultural models of youth.

The critiques raised here bear witness to how the concept of "youth culture" put forward by Parsons and colleagues engenders an essentially static image, distant from the diversity of experiences and contradictions faced by youth. In this manner, that representation ends up annihilating differences and trivialising processes that are doubtless much more complex (Wyn & White, 1997). In so doing, they render coherent a subject – young people – and an object – their cultural models – that eschew a static and homogenising representation and rather, are constantly at pains to revendicate their heterogeneity (Bennett & Kahn-Harris, 2004). "Youth culture" thus becomes a *myth* (Elkin & Westley, 1955; Jahoda & Warren, 1965) and as myth, it covers a specific function: in light of its evocative potential, it guarantees the internal coherence of the elements it is made up of, it makes intelligible every potential crisis, and last but not least, defines reintegration ceremonies.

With these caveats in mind, almost a decade after the publication of the *Adolescent society*, James S. Coleman himself, despite still defending the existence of a "youth culture" and the opportunity and need to examine its peculiar characteristics, came up with a less stringent definition:

> These and other attributes can be said to describe a 'youth culture', not because they constitute a homogeneous culture, nor because they characterize all youth, but because taken together, they are activities initiated by youth and pursued more by youth than by adults (Coleman, 1974: 113).

Despite believing it was "still the case" to talk of youth culture, it is clear that this suggestion tries, at least in part, to overcome the contradictions underlined thus far: therefore, Coleman recalls aspects such as "inward-lookingness" (namely mimicking each other as role models), the "psychic attachment of youth to others their own age" and the growing need for "closeness, intimacy, and extreme openness among a small group of close friends", the tendency toward autonomy, the shifts in communication processes and the growing captivation with the mass media of the time, movies, radio and newspapers, the "concern for the underdog", and above all, the renewed interest in change.

"Youth culture" has revealed itself as a theoretical artifice and an analytical tool that over time has retained an undeniable charm in sociological debate, ending up with becoming almost "common sense" and given-for-granted. From this perspective, the problem is not about accepting or rejecting this concept in an uncritical manner, but rather of putting effort into a theorisation process that can go beyond a merely descriptive perspective (Ardigò, 1966; Allen, 1968). However, it also has to do with exploring other concepts and perspectives, being mindful, as provocatively emphasised by Simon Frith (1984: 64), that:

> It is always tempting to take a set of categories developed to make sense of one historical moment and to apply them to another historical moment, as if sociological concepts had a permanent, ahistorical power.

In relation to this, the concept of youth culture and the research perspectives examined in this Chapter appear to fail to realise that the cultural expressions of the young American students of the 1950s and 1960s weren't only a manifestation of adaptation and consent, but also a testament to mounting dissent (Feixa, 1998[3]; Feixa, Leccardi & Nilan, 2016). That dissent – of which the songs of Joan Baez and Bob Dylan, often guests at Cambridge's *Club 47* (Hajdu, 2001), a few metres from *Department of Social Relations* speak of – represents the key theme around which the research process that will be discussed in the next Chapter takes shapes: a debate instigated by a group of intellectuals and scholars with diverse theoretical and often ideological backgrounds, sharing the desire to develop a reading that could surpass the limits of structural functionalism (Gouldner, 1970), to underscore the profound discontinuities witnessed in youth.

# 4 Youth, dissent and counterculture. The "long 1960s" in Goodman, Keniston, and Roszak

## 4.1. The (un)complacent youth

The events that rocked young people's lives in the "long 1960s" – going roughly from the late 1950s to approximately early 1970s – in North America and Europe shed light on the boundaries of what can be considered, in the collective imagination, as one of the periods of greater visibility and enkindling of youth protagonism. This period was inaugurated by the "invasion" of groups of vagrants embracing what could be called – to quote an iconic novel from the time – an *On the road* culture (Kerouac, 1957) and culminating in the student protests (Lipset, 1968, 1993[2]; Graham, 2006; Fahlenbrach, Klimke & Scharloth, 2016).

It should be noted that the unfolding of events and, above all, the forms of conflict – or rather, to anticipate some of the categories which we will draw upon later, of opposition or dissent – between the adult generation and the younger one have exhibited different features in the United States, Canada, the UK, France, Germany and Italy, to mention but just a few contexts (Hollstein, 1969; Marwick, 2012[2]; Milligan, 2014; Mercer, 2020). While each case is unique, there are nonetheless distinctive aspects that allow to ascribe meaning to a complex event and its medium and long-term effects, as regards the (self)perception of youth cultures and identities.

An episode which can be considered particularly emblematic as it marks a phase of strong opposition, which started with the Berkeley protests, is the occupation of Columbia University in 1968. Among the numerous testimonies of that episode (case in point *The Strawberry Statement* by James Simon Kunen, then adapted to film), is an excerpt by Frederick W. Dupee, literary critic and essayist for *The Partisan Review*, that enables us to re-live those moments:

> I saw the start of the rush to the Park and later in the day, when I went to Hamilton Hall, headquarters of Columbia College, for a 2 P.M. office hour, a sort of sit-in seemed to be developing in the lobby. At that moment the affair looked insignificant. However, coming down about 3:30 I found the crowd much larger and louder. Its spirit was still festive, though: there were guitars, far-out costumes, acrobatics […]. Once out of Hamilton Hall I didn't go back till the following day (Wednesday the 24th). But the radio had brought news of Hamilton's occupation by the Blacks and of the seizure of President Kirk's offices in Low Library by the whites. Hence my reluctance to go to the

Shakespeare class [...]. Nevertheless, I went [...]. Several large windows form a stately row along the second story of that wall. An incredible number of rebel students stood or sat in those windows, while others were climbing up to them, or down from them, by the wrought iron grilles conveniently fixed to the smaller windows on the ground floor (Dupee, 1968).

The long phase of dissent and student protest rekindled the attention devoted to youth culture by the social sciences (Manning & Truzzi, 1972; Silverstein, 1972), renewing – in Sheila Allen's words (1973: 437) – that "mixture of wonder, contempt, fear and romanticism" typical of the adult gaze on young people. Compared to the previous phase, which as argued in the previous Chapter, revolved around the functionalist paradigm and the themes of socialisation and social integration of youth (Musgrove, 1964), a novel, meaningful aspect stands out: the interest of a group of intellectuals and scholars – in large part, but not exclusively, radicals and Marxists – who view this new "invasion" critically, yet at the same time are deeply attracted by the possibilities for cultural change offered by young people's ideals and practices (Lifton, 1968).

Young people become the symbols of a rich, diverse and bright kaleidoscope of colours, sounds and images through which – supported by a group of poets, writers, performers, music groups, artists and intellectuals who sympathetically observe, recount and sustain the *Movement* – they put forward "new ideas, new social concerns and new forms of social participation" (Marwick, 2006: 43). Elements that rapidly spread through the social fabric, define the tastes, symbolic codes and lifestyles able to generate, up to the point of absorption or isolation, an unprecedented influence on the culture of subsequent decades.

The impact of the *Movement* – or perhaps the aura that surrounds it – questions the common representation of youth as "complacent", typical of the 1950s. This is a representation that, as Charles Wright Mills argues in a text originally published in 1958, was shared by all those who "have done so mainly in the direction of private troubles", but fail "in converting uneasiness into explicit troubles". In other words, these are those trapped either in "their own parochial anger" or in "their own unimaginative ambitions" who express a one-sided rage, without being able to connect "private troubles and public images inside a lineup of their own problems" (Mills, 1963: 388; 394).

Consequently, some perceive youth activism as evidence of the affirmation of a new social and political subjectivity (Milligan, 2014). John and Margaret Rowntree's analysis (1968) included in a brief essay translated into various languages, is an example of this. The essay had a far-reaching impact and was then drawn upon by Edgar Z. Friedenberg (1969) in the context of a broader reflection on the reasons fuelling the "generation gap". Young people are described as a new industrial reserve army. They are placed in a position that impairs their productive potential, yet are central to mechanisms of consumption, thus revealing the contradictions of American capitalism and "as happens when a class is exploited, young people are beginning to become aware of their exploitation […] and are available to develop a consciousness of themselves as a class" (Rowntree & Rowntree, 1968: 9). Thus, replacing the proletariat, they are perceived as the new, potentially revolutionary "class".

Once again, it is not about endorsing or identifying a midway interpretation. Rather, it is about becoming aware of how the experience of young people in the "long 1960s" "was not monolithic" (Marwick, 2006: 44), and was rather the product of an elaborate, complex and diverse process. Therefore, in line with the broader aims of the book, the objective of the present Chapter is not – and could not be – that of reproducing the entire debate which took shape in that phase. We shall instead seek to follow, by delving deeper into several contributions to the debate on the season of dissent and youth protest, a trajectory that can help conceptualise the premises, the manifold faces, the most immediate outcomes and consequences of the long period going from the end of the 1950s to the early 1970s.

In particular, we will refer to the contribution of Paul Goodman, Theodore Roszak and, more in detail, Kenneth Keniston: three intellectuals and scholars with different theoretical and methodological backgrounds sharing a sometimes explicit, sometimes covert sympathy for young people and the transformation potential they embody. This will allow us to grasp the main elements and the diversity of experiences, yet also the obsessions and silences (Merico, 2002) that have characterised the debate on young people, dissent and subculture in the "long 1960s".

## 4.2. "Growing up absurd"? Paul Goodman's visionary sociology

In the summer of 1959, a small New York publishing house commissioned to Paul Goodman – intellectual and creative writer focusing on themes such as politics, psychology, democracy, education, and urban planning – a book on teenage gangs, theme at the heart of a vivacious, albeit contradictory *Cycle of Outrage* of the time (Gilbert, 1986). Goodman handed over to the editor a manuscript, that being partly inspired by his previous articles, avoided to directly address the issues raised by the publishing house, but rather suggested a critical reflection on the social and cultural system within which youth were raised. The manuscript was turned down by the publisher. In the first few months of 1960, the monthly magazine *Commentary* published some extracts from the manuscript (Podhoretz, 1967; Stoehr, 1990), that was then printed the following year as *Growing Up Absurd. Problems of Youth in the Organized System* (Goodman, 1960).

The book belongs to the genre of social criticism typical of many works produced in the 1950s (Riesman, 1950a; Whyte, 1956). At the heart of Goodman's critique is the emphasis on prosperity and conformity distinctive of the culture of the affluent post-war 1950s (Goodman, 1966). In this respect, the rise of urban youth gang warfare and the popular portrayal of the non-conformist outsider (suffice it to think about the popularity of movies such as the 1955 *Rebel Without a Cause* and *East of Eden*, and the 1957 *West Side Story*) gave voice to a widespread concern and appeared to symbolise a pervasive sign of an incumbent moral decline. According to Goodman instead, "much in American society undercuts senses of worthwhile work and authentic vocation by a fraudulent emphasis on 'role-playing,' by commercial exploitation, and by rationalisation and perpetuation of a technocratic system for its own sake". In other words, the author's intention was to demonstrate that American society was unable to offer young people the possibility to express their autonomy and creativity, thus preventing them from enjoying "adequate access to genuine activity and to place in a concerned community" (Widmer, 1980: 67–68). According to Goodman, this has led to the rule according to which "with regard to the next generation, everybody always has a higher standard than the one he is used to" loosing traction over time. This is echoed in his stated plan and aim for the book:

> I assume that the young really need a more worth-while world in order to grow up at all, and I confront this real need with the world that they have been getting. This is the source of their problems. Our problem is to remedy the disproportion. We can (Goodman, 1960: xv–xvi).

Goodman's answer revolves around the need to reconfigure a world that he perceives to be inured and bemused, in an attempt to offer new generations novel opportunities. The break with the social sciences and sociology is thereby enacted:

> Our social scientists have become so accustomed to the highly organized and by-and-large smoothly running society that they have begun to think that 'social animal' means 'harmoniously belonging.' They do not like to think that fighting and dissenting are proper social functions, nor that rebelling or initiating fundamental change is a social function. Rather, if something does not run smoothly, they say it has been improperly socialized; there has been a failure in communication (*Ivi*: 10–11).

Signalling a strong discontinuity with the widespread perception of the behaviours and choices of youth as a social problem, the reaction to which ought to be a reminder of the respect owed to societal norms, Goodman maintains that the disaffection manifested by young Americans has to be, instead, understood as a symptom, and is therefore wholly justified: they are in fact, required to grow up in an environment that is incapable to offer adequate responses to their needs and capacities, namely "real opportunities for worthwhile experience" (*Ivi*: 12). Thus, as he meaningfully summarises, the issue at hand is that "it is hard to grow up when existing facts are treated as though they do not exist. For then there is no dialogue, it is impossible […] to make a bridge between oneself and society" (*Ivi*: 39).

Hence, in his book Goodman untangles some of the key challenges faced by the society of his time and teases out the answers put forward by youth culture: "Jobs", "Class structure", "Aptitude", "Patriotism", "Faith" and sexuality.

To describe the functioning of American society, almost evoking the concept of the "iron cage" introduced by Max Weber (1904), Goodman (1960: 160) conjures the metaphor of an "*apparently closed room*" within which a "*rat race*" takes place. This is a race in which all the members of the Organized System should participate. Focusing on youth, Goodman suggests "a fair survey of what disturbed youth is indeed doing: some running that race, some disqualified from running it and hanging around because there is nowhere else, some balking in the race, some attacking the machine, etc.". If we were to summarise the main groups identified by Goodman, we could distinguish four categories. The first category including those who take part in the race and embrace the values and means at their disposal (employed, middle-class youth and conformists). The second comprising those who participate in the race without fully endorsing the modalities or values (marginalised youth lacking education and criminal gangs). The third bringing together those who have willingly abandoned the race: the beats who have rationally given up. Finally, there are those who "direct more vigorous attacks against the machine itself and try to stop it": the English Angry Young Men and the French "existentialist" youth (*Ivi*: 165).

Goodman devotes specific attention to the beats' typical models – that he calls "The early resigned" – and to juvenile delinquents – defined as "The early fatalistic". In his view, while these two categories have different backgrounds, with the first hailing from the middle-class and the second representing the underprivileged, they nonetheless enact practices able to highlight the contradictions of the dominant model (Widmer, 1980). Nonetheless, their critique appears to lack a sufficient degree of (political) maturity, able to produce significant cultural change: on the one hand, the dissent of the beats stops at the level of renunciation and does not translate into an impetus to reform institutions; on the other, "the delinquent fatalism is the feeling of no chance in the past, no prospect for the future, no recourse in the present; whence the drive to disaster" (Goodman, 1960: 211).

In the first pages of the book Goodman poses the question: "Socialization to what?" (*Ivi*: 11). As we have argued, his answer rests on the assumption that the entire socialisation model is intrinsically wrong and should thus be revisited, as it ends up engendering the very symptoms of disaffection which it purported to appease (Fishman, 1975; Stoehr, 1990). In the final chapter he exhorts readers to take on their duty to bring to bear what he terms "missed or compromised fundamental social changes": changes needed to build "The Missing Community" and the relative physical environment, the economic and social spheres, the political reform, as well as improvements pertaining to education and work (Goodman, 1960: 217).

Certainly, as Kingsley Widmer has observed (1980: 70), *Growing Up Absurd* can be deemed as "a sometimes insightful but often ill-organized, cliched, and superficial piece of topical social criticism". Goodman's analyses are sometimes based on dubious definitions and references. The language used is in instances rhetorical. A detailed examination of the condition of young women and of the role of racial conflict is entirely missing. In parts, the analysis dismisses relevant elements. More generally, many of the factors addressed in the book now sound outdated.

Regardless, it is undeniable that the work was pioneering for its time, despite its contribution having been frequently disregarded afterwards. Its main merit resides in all probability in having drawn the attention of public opinion to the need to care about young people and their discontents, well before youth took over campuses (Fishman, 1975). It is worth noting that his "visionary sociology", his anarchic approach, his communitarianism, his references to Oriental mysticism and to the Gestalt doctrine rapidly turned him into an advocate of the counterculture (Roszak, 1969; Widmer, 1980). Despite the difficulties that undergirded its publication (Goodman, 1966), in a short period of time *Growing Up Absurd* turned into "one of the campus bibles of the sixties", and one of the mirrors through which young dissenters viewed themselves (Podhoretz, 1967: 297).

## 4.3. Faces of dissent: From youth alienation to youth protest

Let's turn the clock back to the late 1950s, to look into an analytical perspective able to account for the complex intertwining of the processes of social and political change, the biographical dimension and the sphere of psycho-social development that underlies youthful dissent. During his scientific career, Kenneth

Keniston devoted over a decade to the study of youth and its cultural expressions. In particular, between 1957 and 1971 the social psychologist developed a complex research program that, inspired by Erik H. Erikson's psycho-historical approach, aimed at analysing the relationship between *youth and dissent*, along a continuum that went from *alienation* to *commitment* (Côté, 2014; Furlong, 2017).

Keniston developed his analysis from a re-evaluation of two representations of youth: on one hand, the paradigmatic one of early modernity, which he identified as *apprenticeship for social mobility*, where the main aim of youth was to acquire the qualities and skills needed to successfully cope with adult life (Furlong & Cartmel, 1997); on the other, the one typical of the period between the end of the 1940s and the early 1960s, namely – as we saw in the previous Chapter – the phase of *youth culture* (Parsons, 1942, 1962), of which he emphasises in particular the dimension of *"privatism"* (Riesman, 1950a). Although they have emerged in subsequent historical moments and while considering their mutual differences and internal diversifications, according to Keniston, these two (*traditional*) conceptions of youth had a common foundation: both, in fact, defined young people as indifferent and apathetic. In this way, they prevented or stopped any kind of social and political commitment.

The mobilisations that rocked the US campuses in the early 1960s led him to noticing some contradictory signs, i.e. a mounting youth engagement that could not be understood through the prism of the two conceptions of youth described above. Even if somewhat emphatically, he pointed out that, compared to previous cohorts, students entering colleges in that phase seemed to be well prepared, more sensitive to the expressive dimensions of educational processes, much more aware of the need to take their future in their own hands. In his opinion, these elements designated the emergence of a third representation of youth, which he suggested to define as *academic*. This conception

> has as its distinctive feature a commitment to intellect, to knowledge, to scholarship and the academic enterprise, relatively unheard of in earlier American college generations. At the same time, it involves considerable generational self-consciousness (Keniston, 1962/1963: 93).

They were students who combined a strong academic interest with a new style of political commitment – cautious, restrained, reflective –which unfolded in the search for new strategies to implement the values transmitted by their parents.

Marking a point of strong discontinuity with some of the analyses dedicated to youth in that period, the American scholar highlighted the need to pay attention to the plural expressions of youth culture and, consequently, defining the phenomenon broadly enough to include all its manifestations. In particular,

Keniston (1965, 1969a) showed how the tensions that had rocked the American campuses in the late 1960s could not be interpreted in the light of a single array of factors (psychological, institutional, historical or political) and, above all, could not be ascribed to some sort of unity (the *"Movement"*) capable of coherently containing all the manifestations. From his writings, there emerges the awareness of the internal plurality and differences (in terms of values, background and personality types) between the different groups and the different types that animated and accompanied the rise of that youthful *new opposition*.

Here lies the theoretical foundation of the research carried out by Keniston. In its theorisation, dissent could not be understood except in terms of an intrinsically *plural* phenomenon. In particular, he insisted on emphasising the multiplicity of the *"faces"* through which dissent manifested itself in the experiences of the youths of the 1960s (Keniston, 1966). Nevertheless, the empirical analysis and the observation of those forms of youth dissent offered – in his opinion – the chance of outlining a more general theoretical model, useful to interpret this plurality within a *continuum*, where the extremes are two ideal types of dissent: on the one hand, the *disaffiliated*; and on the other, the *political activist* (Touraine, 1974[2]). The result is an articulated and detailed reconstruction of some of the *faces of dissent* that took stage in that controversial season: first of all, the *alienated* and the *radicals*, followed by the *dropouts, the drug users* and *idealists*. In the next few pages, the first two types will be discussed in greater detail, followed by a brief reconstruction of the other three *faces* suggested, which have been the focus of smaller studies.

The first form of dissent analysed by Keniston is that of *alienation*. He focused, in particular, on university students who had assumed an "uncommitted" attitude or repudiation towards the culture that surrounded them, thus highlighting an explicit "rejection" of American values. In his opinion, this was a "new" form of alienation, typical of young intellectuals, which could not be understood as something "imposed", but rather as the result of "choice". The novelty of this conceptualisation of alienation is twofold, because, on the one hand, it emerges in a new type of society and, on the other, it takes on a shape that can be emblematically represented with the icon of Nicholas Ray's *Rebel without a cause* (played by James Dean). It is therefore an alienation that affects young people in the middle and upper strata of society and that is capable of offering a response to the pressures and tensions instigated by society.

Under the guidance of Henry A. Murray and with the support of Alden Wessman, David Ricks and Arthur Couch, between 1957 and 1962, Keniston developed an extensive research project, the results of which are discussed in *The Uncommitted. Alienated youth in American society* (1965). According to the

American scholar, the alienation of those students implied a specific attitude towards the usual activities and a well-defined *lifestyle*. This style was characterised by an intense intellectual drive, a propensity toward study that went beyond the strictly academic content, the search for extracurricular activities capable of giving expression to artistic and aesthetic interests, the persistent adoption of the role of "detached observer" (Touraine, 1974[2]: 238) and, above all, by a proneness to examine in an almost compulsive way the relationships with others along an incessant "searching for motives, meanings, and effects" of one's own actions.

According to Keniston (1965: 97, 103), these were subjects who, in the absence of clear criteria giving them direction, renounced to choose and wandered constantly in search of their own self, paying the price for their opposition to the values and models of society with a sense of "inner confusion, disunity, and fragmentation" of identity. In addition, the attention of the alienated youth goes almost exclusively toward the "cult of the present", which corresponds to the perception of the past as meaningless and the entrenchment of pessimism towards the future and of doubt concerning his own planning skills. Overall, the cases analysed revealed that at the basis of the alienation of these students was – Keniston stated (*Ivi*: 199) – a "repudiation of conventional pathways to adulthood", perceived "as asking a price that they are unable and unwilling to pay".

More generally, in line with his other works on dissent, the alienation of the students he interviewed can be fully grasped only if it is considered as an expression of the interweaving of individual and social factors. It follows that alienation "is a response by selectively predisposed individuals to dilemmas and problems that confront our entire society" (*Ivi*: 205). The alienated must therefore be considered, at the same time, products of and rebels against this society.

The alienated are understood by Keniston as *innovators* (Merton, 1949[2]): the deviance that they express is meant as a vital resource for their culture, because, instead of representing a pathological dimension, in their *"atypical"* personal development it is possible to identify new responses to the contradictions of society, which their *"typical"* peers – those who identify themselves in the "youth culture" – cannot observe. Thus, their presence helps to recognise new cracks and inconsistencies in the social and biographical organisation. However, if alienation allows to identify the contradictions of a type of society, where some of the most talented young people retire to private life, "the most contractive potential for social improvement is thereby lost" together with the possibility of a radical critique of the *status quo* (Keniston, 1965: 417).

The second type of dissent analysed by Keniston is that of the *activist*, with particular reference to the research he carried out in the summer of 1967, the results of which are discussed in *Young radicals. Notes on committed youth* (1968a). The subject of the research was a group of young radical students engaged in the *Vietnam Summer*. Keniston did not focus on the organisational, functioning or influential forms of that organisation, but rather on the political socialisation and biographical and identity construction of its young leaders. In such manner, the book assumes the characteristics of a *collective biography* imbued – Keniston said (*Ivi*: 44) – with the will to combine the attempt to "formulate what these radicals brought in common from their own past" with the desire to highlight the deep variety of the experiences of those young people, their stories, the roots of their commitment.

In his analysis, Keniston distanced himself from those who interpreted the (personal) roots of the radicalism of young people either by emphasising their discontinuity with the past, or underlining the dimension of intergenerational continuity. In this sense, the radicalisation of the *Vietnam Summer* leaders must be understood as a process rather than a point of arrival, an evolving style rather than a definite identity or a stable ideology. In this process, Keniston argued, aspects of change and signals of intergenerational continuity coexisted. That is – to evoke the categories of Erikson (1963) – elements of *fidelity* and *diversity* intersected. However, as the American psychologist highlighted, the experience enabled participants to realise the rising levels of social injustice, become aware of the ineffectiveness of the System and appropriate the consequent search for a *new interpretation* of society. Unlike their peers, after having solved the crisis of anxieties, the feelings of guilt, the unhappiness typical of early adolescence, young radicals experience a second identity crisis (Erikson 1968). This new crisis has its roots in their dissatisfaction for the balance reached at the end of adolescence: it is precisely that sense of dissatisfaction and frustration that leads them to collectively embrace the aspiration towards "radical" changes. The next step is their "activation" and adherence to a collective path where everyone is "personally responsible for effecting radical changes" leading to new patterns of behaviour and self-reflection concerning their effectiveness (Keniston, 1968a: 110).

Here we can therefore highlight the core of his representation of the *activist*: a subject who can no longer make a distinction between the effort of personal transformation and the attempt to create a radical movement; but also a subject whose identity is defined as being in constant dialogue with the dilemmas between "encapsulation and solidarity, participation and power, process and program, and cultural and political revolution" that characterised the composite universe of the New Left (*Ivi*: 190–191).

Despite being a minority in the American student movement, the leaders of the *Vietnam Summer* interpreted two peculiar aspects of that society in transformation. In the first instance, they manifested a sense of openness and readiness towards the future, which they perceived as "open, fluid, undefined and indeterminate" (*Ivi*: 41). Secondly, they built their own lives upon the premise of constant openness to change, thus assuming as their individual horizon what will become, in the course of a few decades, a breeding ground for the shared political identity of young people (Berger, Berger & Kellner, 1974; Beck & Beck-Gernsheim, 2001).

The typical features of the radical identity type (the openness, the refusal of lasting commitments, the distance from adult roles, the choice not to engage with institutions) were – however – inevitably *temporary*. It was, in other words, an identity destined to take on a more definite characterisation (whether due to stable work and family roles or becoming a radical "professional"). However, it also could be maintained that to an extent those *activists* find themselves occupying "a curious position between adolescence and adulthood" (Keniston, 1968a: 259).

Beyond these two dominant types, Keniston examines other three *faces* of juvenile dissent, that position themselves midway along the previously-mentioned continuum, each with their own distinctive features which we will unpack shortly.

The first profile he focused on is that of *dropouts*, the boy or girl who leave college or university in a quest for their true selves outside of an institutional context. According to Keniston, in the choice of the *dropout* lies the ambivalent combination of a "desire for a sense of autonomy and control" and the "need to see their behavior as defiant and rebellious". It is above all a way to create a distance from the pressures of the "typical" student and elaborate an adaptive response, allowing to identify new opportunities to define a new self (Keniston & Hirsch, 1970: 211–212).

The second type analysed is that of *drug users*. Keniston (1968/1969) pinpointed three different forms: *tasters, seekers* and *acid heads*. In his opinion, the use of drugs and the modes of consumption could not be interpreted as an aspect linked exclusively to the psychology of the individual. What emerged from his analysis was, rather, the sense that

> student drug use […] is above all an indirect criticism of our society's inability to offer the young exciting, honourable, and effective ways of using their intelligence and idealism to reform our society (*Ivi*: 252).

The third type analysed is that of the *idealists*. In contrast to the positions advocated by many of his academic colleagues, in his opinion high moral development was not sufficient to account for the involvement of young people in the various protests, sit-ins and clashes. He argued that the studies carried out indicate that:

> those who have reached higher levels of moral development are more likely to act in the service of their principles – protesting when their principles are at issue; refusing, also for reasons of principle, to take part in other protest and forms of activism (Keniston, 1970: 261).

In other words, Keniston shows how the response to the paradox between idealism and nihilism could be identified, from time to time, only in the condition of observing the psychological dimension in its relationship with other dimensions of biographical, historical, political and social development.

Doubtless, it is important to mention that Keniston reserved limited and liminal attention to the broader debate that the political and social scientists of the time were grappling with (Habermas et al., 1961; Lipset, 1968). To this, one should add the lack of depth granted to the comparison between young American students and youth hailing from other geographical contexts (Gitlin, 1972); as well as the rather meagre consideration given to the gender dimension (Griffin, 1993) and to the theme of social stratification. This being said, he never concealed – not unlike Robert J. Lifton and Robert Bellah – his sympathy towards the young people he had interacted with and their drive for innovation. It can thus be argued that by identifying the different *faces* of youth dissent which were present and active in American society in the 1960s, Keniston accomplishes an intrinsically cultural effort. That of the young people he speaks of is a constructive dissent, which condemns the generalised apathy towards the others and that is based on critical spirit, a sense of civic responsibility, and on political participation. All qualities that – in his view – must be developed and encouraged, also because they are based on principles that are the basis of an approach to reality which allows to cultivate young people's critical thinking, as well as advocate for the values they believe in.

This is a pivotal theoretical (and political) theme that will be addressed by various intellectuals, including Theodore Roszak, and which we will turn to in the next paragraph, as it is an emblematic example of a widespread attitude in the 1960s.

## 4.4. Roszak and "The Making of a Counter Culture"

In 1969, Theodore Roszak – history lecturer and American novelist – published *The Making of a Counter Culture*, a passionate analysis of youth dissent in the 1960s, some sections of which had been written for the magazine *The Nation*.

More than for the contents of the analysis, the relevance of the book resides first and foremost in having encouraged and supported a strong identity definition: almost replicating the path forged in *Growing up absurd*, Roszak's book immediately captured, in fact, the attention of a vast audience of young protesters, dropouts, and rebels. As sociologist Todd Gitlin (president of *Students for a Democratic Society* between 1963 and 1964) used to recall, the book set a useful framework to grasp the collective meaning of the experiences of a multitude of young people. It offered a name, a shared and shareable label, that of "counter culture", to something young people were trying to figure out (Duncan, 2013).

The term was by no means new in the social sciences debate. Specifically referring to delinquency and more generally to the behaviour of adolescents, in a famous essay published in the *American Sociological Review*, J. Milton Yinger had, in fact, already suggested using the concept of "contraculture" – juxtaposing it to that of "subculture" – "to call attention to the conflict aspects" of the phenomena that were being studies (Yinger, 1960: 629, n. 10). In particular, Yinger claims that:

> the use of the term contraculture [... should be privileged] wherever the normative system of a group contains, as a primary element, a theme of conflict with the values of the total society, where personality variables are directly involved in the development and maintenance of the group's values, and wherever its norms can be understood only by reference to the relationships of the group to a surrounding dominant culture (*Ivi*: 629).

This interpretation aids us in contextualising the analysis made in *The Making of a Counter Culture*. Early in the book, Roszak (1969: 4) asserts: "the paramount struggle of our day is against a far more formidable, because far less obvious, opponent, to which I will give the name 'the technocracy' ". He argues that the emergence of that "social form" – rooted in ideals such as modernising, rationalising, planning and on imperatives such as efficiency, social security, and affluence – was gradually dehumanising society and engendering a process of large-scale alienation of individuals, particularly young people. In the light of this, *The Making of a Counter Culture* was perceived – almost embodying the suggestion made by Ortega y Gasset (1923), mentioned in the opening of the second chapter of Roszak's book – as a scenario that "far more than merely 'meriting' attention, desperately requires it". The "ebullient culture of youthful dissent" offered, as Roszak (1969: 34) repeatedly claimed, a "matrix in which an alternative, but still excessively fragile future is taking shape"; an innovation "that might transform this disoriented civilization of ours into something a human being can identify as home" (*Ivi*: xii–xiii). It outlined, ultimately, "a culture [...] radically disaffiliated from the main stream assumptions of our society" (*Ivi*: 42).

Roszak (1969: 1) was aware that those supporting "what is presently happening that is new, provocative, and engaging in politics, education, the arts, social relations", were only a negligible minority of young people. Yet he does not hold back from emphasising how, in his view, that avantgarde could help drag the rest. His optimism was motivated by a few basic considerations: the rising number of young people relative to the total population; the spread of higher education and the consequent increase of their cultural capital; the possibility to cement the unity and solidarity of groups through shared living arrangements for young people on university campuses – that he compares to the "dark satanic mills of early industrialism" (*Ivi*: 28); and more generally, the perception that young people were becoming more and more cognisant of their role in society.

In his analysis, Roszak teases out some key features allowing to identify the common denominator that in his view can give wholeness and unity back to the counter cultural variety comprising reactions to McCarthyism, protests against the Vietnam War, the radicalisation of the civil rights movement, the new feminist movement, up to those reacting to the Watergate scandal. First and foremost, the persistent references to categories like "revolution", "experience", "fantasy" and above all "imagination": keywords that – as emblematically testified by the slogan displayed at the entrance of the University of Sorbonne in 1968 "*We are inventing a new and original world. Imagination is seizing power*" – echoed in American and European squares and universities. To this, one should add the questioning of the themes and mechanisms of the Age of Affluence: the family, work, education, success, cis-gender relations, sexuality, technology, and progress. Thirdly, the symbolic relevance of typical themes constituting the cultural base of young bohemians: "new types of community, new family patterns, new sexual mores, new kinds of livelihood, new esthetic forms, new personal identities" (*Ivi*: 69). Last but by no means least, the recurrent references to a rich array of political, cultural and intellectual underpinnings, which Roszak analyses in the central part of the book: "The dialectics of liberation" that emerge from the Freudian Marxism of Herbert Marcuse and the mysticism of Norman Brown; the songs of Bob Dylan; the New Left sociology of Mills; the "Journey to the East" of Allen Ginsberg and Alan Watts; "The use and abuse of psychedelic experience"; Paul Goodman's visionary utopia; Timothy Leary's occult narcissism.

Roszak is well aware of the elements of marked discontinuity that characterise, as shown in the previous paragraph, the different personalities of the counterculture (Keniston, 1968a, 1971), particularly the most politically-charged and violent, and the pacificist and alienated fringes respectively:

When one first casts an eye over the varieties of youthful dissent, it may seem that there is considerably less coherence to this counter culture than I have suggested. […] The tension one senses between these two movements is real enough.

Nonetheless, he states:

> I think there exists, at a deeper level, a theme that unites these variations and which accounts for the fact that hippy and student activist continue to recognize each other as allies (Roszak, 1969: 62).

Ultimately, he identifies – and in ways urges to unearth – a common ground, shared by the radical students and hippie dropouts of the 1960s, who had joined forces in what Herbert Marcuse (1964) had called the "Great Refusal". As already mentioned in this Chapter's opening, this common ground is rooted in their mutual rejection of what he calls the technocracy – the common enemy – and expresses itself in the joint call for an appreciation of human "sensibility".

A historiographical evaluation of Roszak's interpretation or of the validity of the unity he strived for, is well beyond the scope of this book. Nonetheless, it is worth pointing out that the pages of *The Making of a Counter Culture* stand out for a style in which the analysis of social and historical events on the one hand, and idealistic and political stances on the other, inextricably intersect, almost overlapping: until the point – as in the last chapter of Roszak's book – that the tone adopted stops short of mysticism.

> This, so I have argued, is the primary project of our counter culture: to proclaim a new heaven and a new earth so vast, so marvelous that the inordinate claims of technical expertise must of necessity withdraw in the presence of such splendor to a subordinate and marginal status in the lives of men (Roszak, 1969: 240).

The emerging circumstances, facts, and positions are celebrated, even beyond their historical value, while others are dismissed, ending up omitting an articulate collection of values, symbols and meanings that nonetheless characterised that season of youth cultures. However, conscious of the precariousness of that "strategy of strategies" that spoke to a lack of long-term organisation, and "despite the fraudulence and folly that collects around its edges", Roszak (1969: 38) appears to manifest a near unconditional faith in the abilities and most of all, in the implicit innovative potential of that "new culture a-borning among our youth" during (and as a reaction to) the Age of Affluence. In the backdrop, there is still a consistent personal involvement bringing the scholar closer to the object of analysis. As he himself underscored, 25 years after his first publication of *The Making of a Counter Culture*:

One of its principal values is the contemporary perspective it provides. This is how things looked to one participant-observer in the midst of the upheaval. I hope I captured something of the idealism and adventure of the time – at least as they could be conveyed in the words and thoughts of its most influential minds (Roszak, 1995: 34).

## 4.5. A "postmodern youth"

Drawing on the research he conducted, Keniston highlights how the different forms of youth opposition, which emerged in the 1960s, share the cultural and psychological traits of a *new* generation. The social psychologist's take is that it is the first " 'postmodern' generation". This generation cannot be defined in ideological, political or pragmatic terms. On the contrary, what identifies it is the "slow emergence of a youthful style" (Keniston, 1968b: 288), which denotes in a new manner the ways in which these young people relate to their own experience (Arnett, 2004). This effectively means that the elements able to condition a shared generational belonging must first be looked for, in this perspective, in the *lifestyle* adopted by young people in the context of their experience (Berzano & Genova, 2015).

Taking a leaf out of Robert J. Lifton's book (1968, 1993), Keniston (1968a: 287 *ff.*) puts forward a profile of *post-modern style* hinging on the following features: *fluidity, change* and *movement*; *generational identification* and *inclusion*; *personalism* and *participation*; a pronounced *ambivalence toward technology*; adherence to *non-violence*; finally, the *search for new forms of adulthood, orientation to the future, values, styles of human interaction, ways of knowing, types of social organisation, concepts of man* and *society*.

The emergence of a *postmodern style* manifests itself in conjunction with a deep transformation in the organisation of the life path. Not unlike the 20th century trajectory described by Hall (1904) in relation to adolescence, he argued that the changes taking place were beginning to provide a growing number of individuals with the possibility of a post-adolescent stage of psychological development (Keniston, 1968a). This new stage situates itself in between adolescence and adulthood: these are subjects, who despite having overcome the typical adolescent crisis, still haven't found a satisfactory answer to their questions about the relationship with society, professional rank, social roles and lifestyles that in the past governed entry into adulthood (Arnett, 2004). Although they are no longer adolescents and even if "they fulfill most of the psychological criteria of adulthood" – Keniston highlights (1968a: 260) – those subjects "lack the prime sociological characteristic of adulthood: 'integration' into the institutional structures of society". He suggests to refer to this new stage of life by employing the category of "youth" despite being aware of the need of "assigning to this venerable but vague term a new and specific meaning" (Keniston, 1971: 7). Let us tease out its distinctive traits.

Like other stages of life, it is a *transition* phase, stemming from the transformations experienced by the individual in the previous phases and is a "preface for further transformations that may (or may not) occur in later life". More generally, Keniston stresses (*Ivi:* 17 *ff.*), it is a psychological and – we may add – sociological stage that generally does not exhaust itself with belonging to specific groups, roles, organisations, classes or social positioning. Similarly, it is difficult to delineate its identity boundaries. At the same time, while mostly coming to the fore in developed countries, youth is not the exclusive prerogative of these countries. It does not represent a universal phase either: it is, according to this interpretation, an "optional" stage of unclear duration that particularly when subjects relying on a richer and more articulated repository of cultural resources are concerned, adds on to adolescence, and becomes a – possible and potential – additional moment for a *"psycho-social moratorium"*, progressively "more protracted and diffuse to the degree that the possibilities for personal becoming are themselves differentiated and indeterminate" (Abrams, 1982: 255).

To the elements that set it apart from other phases of life, we must add the ones that qualify in a specific manner postmodern youth. The first guess – Keniston underscores (1968a: 267) – is to intend it as "a state of mind, a set of questions, and a trajectory of psychological change". In a scenario offering multiple potential options, these subjects choose to indulge in an additional phase of exploration (Arnett, 2004), based on the awareness that:

> in a society changing at an accelerating rate, the longest possible delay before taking the leap into some specific social role may simply be the better part of wisdom. A prolonged survey of the social scene provides that much more time to see how things are shaping up before placing a bet on the future. For all these reasons, some of those who reach the end of adolescence actively seek to postpone entry into the System (Keniston, 1968a: 266).

Keniston (1971: 8 *ff.*) identifies six major themes useful to pin down the psychological and cultural profile of *postmodern youth*.

The first is the manifestation of a *"tension between self and society"*: while adolescents still haven't developed a clear image of themselves and appear to – tacitly – accept the stereotypical representations that are passed on to them by society, young people have already developed their identity and do not accept the incongruence between their own self-conception and the social order.

The second element links back to the *"pervasive ambivalence"* influencing the attempt to render congruent the visions of the self and society, as well as the potential manifestation of a conflict between the maintenance of personal integrity and the achievement of effectiveness in society. In addition, there exists a *"wary probe"* of the adult world through which young people challenge their vulnerability and strength, their integrity and resilience, their abilities and the opportunities that society offers.

The third aspect is the *"refusal of socialization and acculturation"*, which are "self-critically analyzed" in the (ambivalent) attempt to truncate the bonds with the culture, history and roles of belonging. Moreover, the "emergence of *youth-specific identities* and roles", in contrast both with the more transient adolescent enthusiasm and with more stable adult commitments, is emphasised. Regardless of their persistence over time and their hold, these identities and roles have an "inherently temporary" character, which is destined to transform over time.

The fifth element is connected with "the enormous value placed upon change, transformation, and *movement*". Whether referring to their own self, others (in political or social terms) or to geographic and social mobility, young people display – according to Keniston – a sort of "devotion to change" and an "abhorrence of stasis": these are signs of vigorous vitality, that dwindles in the transition to adulthood.

Finally, Keniston says – and this is where Roszak (1969) comes into play again – there is a shared adhesion to the *youthful counterculture*, characterised by a "deliberate cultural distance from the existing social order". Keniston concludes that since in the course of this phase of life, horizontal forms of solidarity take on a primary role, youth countercultures assume growing importance on a par with the growth in the number of subjects entering *postmodern youth*.

The latter is therefore a supplementary stage of life geared toward exploration, that if on the one hand offers individuals an additional opportunity for development, preparing them for entry into adulthood (Keniston, 1969b), on the other hand becomes especially relevant for society as – Keniston points out (1971: 3) – it makes young people "potential members or architects of a better [… society] than ours". Concurrently, without ignoring potential caveats, the overall interpretation allows to emphasise how – from the observation of the "interaction between a peculiar stage of development […, the *postmodern youth*,] and an historical situation that contains new contradictions and ambiguities" (*Ivi*: x) – elements of definite interest, including for the analysis of dissent as expressed by young people in the 1960s, can emerge.

## 4.6. Fury, symbol, value

In 1962, the Italian anthropologist Ernesto de Martino published a collection of articles, which included a text on the destructive fury of Swedish young people in the mid-1950s, reproducing the attitudes of the teddy boys (Feixa, 1998[3], 2020). In response to some of the criticisms received on his conduct in scientific research, which was always balancing methodological rigour and the critique of power (Merico, 2000; Geisshuesler, 2021), De Martino (1962[3]) titles the collection: *Furore, simbolo, valore* (*Fury, Symbol, Value*). Three key elements that can also be invoked to reflect around important issues arising from the works of Goodman, Roszak and Keniston, addressed in this Chapter.

Let's start from the theme of *fury*. First of all, the term conjures the image of an era – the "long 1960s" – which, as stated at the start of this Chapter, symbolises in the collective imagination the explosive outburst of young people's behaviours: from pure destructive fury – as De Martino called it – to the marches and sit-ins of young university students. Nevertheless, here the reference to fury is understood as a sign of urgency – almost an urgency to say, to prove and enhance the value of young people's role – which is recurrent in the pages of the works mentioned in this Chapter, as well as more generally pervasive in discussions by and on young people (Lapassade & Rousselot, 1998). This urgency, in some cases, is such that it shows a glimpse of rather patent traces of a utopian inclination and zealous enthusiasm. More generally, both for Goodman, Roszak and Keniston, that fury manifests itself in an ill-concealed sense of sympathy – a shared feeling – towards the dissenting young people with whom they interact and their drive for innovation. Case in point is Roszak's profile outlined by Richard L. Rapson (1971: xi–xii) in the *Introduction* to *The cult of youth in middle-class America*:

> Theodore Roszak, an historian a little too old and too intellectual to be counted one with the student radicals, but a little too radical to belong to The Establishment, follows with his intriguing new analysis of the 'counter culture' of youth, an analysis that is definitely, but not uncritically, sympathetic to the efforts of the young.

The second aspect that we wish to recall in these concluding lines is articulated in relation to the dimension of the *symbol*, intended in an anthropological sense – De Martino argues (1962[3]) – as evidence of a new reference framework to reconfigure fury and give novel meaning to the experience from which it stems. One should certainly not overlook the contradictions that have afflicted this historical phase of youth culture, which ought to be collectively examined with caution. However, if one looks beneath the surface to find the "core" of all the different forms of dissent characterising that experience (Hollstein, 1969), what emerges is a clear representation of youth that presents itself and is depicted as a symbol of the ambivalent dynamics upsetting the social fabric: it embodies, in other words, both the fears, and the drive for more profound innovation. This is a representation that is present, albeit approached from different perspectives, in the work of both Goodman and Roszak – being they themselves, as we have posited, symbols for that whole generation – as well as, more thoroughly, in the pathway between alienation and protest described by Keniston.

Finally, let's turn to the question of *value*. As we have repeatedly emphasised, the contributions on which we have drawn in this Chapter cannot and do not seek to exhaust the array of issues that characterise the emergence of youth (counter)culture in the 1960s. The aim of the analysis that we have attempted to develop was, rather, to define a trajectory: that very same trajectory that leads from the rise of youth dissent to its more visible, explosive manifestation, whilst also making sure to document its multiple and constantly shifting dimensions, as well as the theories that are useful to study the phenomenon. Doubtless, in the works analysed herein there are elements that have been undervalued, chiefly gender and class-related matters (Griffin, 1993). Nonetheless, the three authors considered forge their analysis of youth dissent within a perspective that eludes traditional disciplinary boundaries, paving the way for a marked interdisciplinary approach (Wyn & Cahill, 2015). This allows them to take as a reference the interdependency between individual, society, power and culture, thus anticipating some key aspects of what will come to be known as the *cultural turn* in the humanities and social sciences (Chaney, 1994).

While they may fall short of offering the contemporary reader theoretical or methodological elements that can be immediately implemented, their main lasting value continues to lie in their ability to elicit a critical approach, that is never complacent and most of all, never overindulgent when it comes to young people and youth cultures.

# 5 Rituals, resistance and style. The CCCS and youth subcultures

## 5.1. A new research agenda

In a short text co-authored with Tony Jefferson and John Clarke, Stuart Hall has argued that *"youth as a concept is unthinkable"*. In the typically provocative style of his works, this statement speaks to the critical reflection on the topic of youth subcultures developed by the *Centre for Contemporary Cultural Studies* at the University of Birmingham (henceforth CCCS). At the heart of this reflection is the acknowledgement that conceptualising youth as a specific "stage of life" has limited sociological relevance (Hall, Jefferson & Clarke, 1976). In other words, the insistence on representing youth "as a single, homogeneous group" sheds light, in their view, on the obsession of those who view age "as the most significant factor of social stratification" (quoted in Devlin, 2006: 2). Above all, it risks becoming an ideological tool that diverts the attention away from other variables – first and foremost, class – that according to CCCS scholars, contribute to the definition of the social positioning of individuals, and relatedly, to their experiences and trajectories.

The CCCS was founded in 1964 by Richard Hoggart to "inaugurate research in the area of contemporary culture and society", with a particular focus on research themes such as "cultural forms, practices and institutions", and an emphasis on "their relation to society and social change" (Hall et al., 1980[3]: vi).

When in 1968, Hoggart resigned from his role at the *Centre* to join UNESCO, Hall took over as Director, a position he covered until 1979. At the time, the CCCS could count on a handful of staff members and research fellows, supported by a few dozen post-graduate research students working on specific projects. Nevertheless, their studies had and continue to have a decisive impact on the international scientific debate, laying the foundations for contemporary *cultural studies* (Couldry, 2000; Miller, 2001; McRobbie, 2005; Walton, 2008).

In Hall's approach (1980a, 1980b), cultural studies should task themselves with defining the contours and at the same time, accentuating the connections between the "two paradigms" that influenced the CCCS' agenda under Hall's aegis: on the one hand, the seeds of what Richard Johnson (1979) has termed *culturalism*, namely a less elitist vision of culture, as put forward, albeit with slightly different connotations, in the works of Hoggart, Raymond Williams and Edward P. Thomson (Hall, 1990); on the other hand, the shift towards *structuralism*, particularly semiotic theory as expounded by Claude Lévi-Strauss and Roland Barthes, and Marxist theory as conceptualised by Louis Althusser (Procter, 2004; Williams, 2011). The necessary tools to *articulate* the two perspectives are offered, as Hall (1980a) points out, by the works of Antonio Gramsci, considered relevant less for his political perspective and more in terms of method and the concept of "hegemony".

Accordingly, the research conducted between 1968 and 1979 unfolds at the intersections of literary studies, linguistics, social history, sociology and cultural anthropology, investigating matters related to *"popular culture"* and spanning topics like music and soccer, fiction and art, television and mass media, education, work, and even race (Gray et al., 2007).

The research project on post-war youth subcultures, developed by the CCCS as of 1972, is to be understood against this backdrop. Likening this research pathway to the one that fathered *Policing the crisis* (Hall et al., 1978), James Procter (2004) contends that it is rooted in the debate which took hold of British public opinion after the mugging of an Irish labourer by three youths of mixed ethnic background. An episode that, in a very short time frame, became emblematic of the anxieties and fears underpinning the social and cultural change affecting Great Britain in the early 70s, wherein the rise of youth (sub)cultures was one of its most peculiar and contradictory manifestations. In all its various theorisations, the project on subcultures sought to observe the life conditions and cultural models of working-class young people grappling with the profound economic crisis which marred Great Britain in those years. Moreover, it wished to highlight the discrepancies between the ways in which young people themselves experienced such events and the practices of "signification" put in place by the press and public opinion (Feixa, 1998[3]; Procter, 2004). In sum, the research carried out by the young scholars at the CCCS "was concerned *both* to examine, concretely and in depth, one 'region' of contemporary culture *and* to understand how this could be connected in an explanatory, non-reductive way, to broader cultural and social structures" (Hall & Jefferson, 2006: viii).

Within an organisational context that existed in a broader anti-authoritarian and anti-establishment climate by which the CCCS was inspired, the project on subcultures was developed collectively by a group bringing together professors, researchers and young graduates (Schulman, 1993) which included, John Clarke, Tony Jefferson, Brian Roberts, Iain Chambers and Angela McRobbie. Joining in the effort were other members of the *Centre* like Paul E. Willis, Dick Hebdige, Rachel Powell, Jenny Garber and Chas Critcher, who nonetheless did not take part regularly in the activities of the "Subcultures Group".

As was underscored on its 30th anniversary "the aim of the Subcultures Group was to provide a common point of reference for the grouping of the Centre's individual graduate research projects examining various aspects of the 'youth culture' phenomenon". The Subcultures Group was thus conceived as "a space for discussion, debate and orientation for these projects; it 'collectivised' background reading, helped to integrate the Centre's programme of work around common themes and facilitated a process of 'grounded theorising' " (Hall & Jefferson, 2006: viii).

This was an effort that did not exhaust itself with the research phase, but was expanded upon via a range of different analyses and the publication of results. In fact, the materials produced in the course of three years of work were first published in the form of stencilled papers – for collective discussion – and then gathered in 1975, in a double volume of the *Working Papers in Cultural Studies*, the CCCS journal. The following year, the same materials were edited in *Resistance through rituals*, a book originally published by Hutchinson and edited by Hall and Jefferson (1976[3]) with contributions from scholars like Paul Corrigan, Simon Frith, Geoffrey Pearson, John Twohig, Graham Murdock, Robin McCron and Steve Butters.

## 5.2. Theoretical foundations

Ken Gelder (2007: 5 *ff.*) has defined that of subculture as a long "vagabond history", that has its roots in the underworld of Elizabethan England, and manifests itself through the characters populating London described by Henry Mayhew, as well as at a later stage in the "mosaic" of idiosyncratic worlds of Chicago studied by Park, Burgess and their students. It's precisely to the students of the Chicago School, first and foremost in light of their specific attention to various forms of urban marginalisation and their ethnographic attitude, that the birth of empirical research on urban subcultures is attributed (Frith, 1984; Brake, 1985; Gelder & Thornton, 1997; Williams, 2011). An excerpt of the introduction to *Profane culture*, where Paul Willis (1978: 1–2) appears to almost re-evoke the words of Robert E. Park, is emblematic in this regard:

> But it is only in the factories, on the streets, in the bars, in the dance halls, in the tower flats, in the two-up-and-two-downs that contradictions and problems are *lived through* to particular outcomes. It is in these places where direct experience, ways of living, creative acts and penetrations – cultures – redefine problems, break the stasis of meaning, and reset the possibilities somewhat for all of us. […] Life is the laboratory. Life is the thing. Ethnography is not simply description, it's about capturing that.

Although in the works of the Chicago School (Cressey, 1932a[2]; Thrasher, 1927[2]) there had already been a first (implicit) mapping of the concept, the first definition was put forward by Milton M. Gordon (Fine & Kleinman, 1979; Williams, 2011). According to the American sociologist, a subculture is nothing more than a "sub-division of a national culture", to which subjects sharing the same social situation (such as class status, ethnic background, rural or urban residence, and religious affiliation) refer to. A subculture is capable of defining a "functioning unity" thus producing an "integration effect" on individuals who participate in it. It is – as Gordon (1947: 41) put it, setting the scene for subsequent studies – "a world within a world".

From then onwards, the concept of subculture has received remarkable attention in sociology (Yinger, 1960) and has been employed on multiple occasions in research on young people, even prior to the theorisation made in Birmingham in the 1970s (Smith, 1976; Jenks, 2005). Worthy of mention are: David Riesman's work (1950b) on youth audience in "Listening to Popular Music"; Albert K. Cohen's (1955) work on youth gang's "delinquent subculture"; the references made by James S. Coleman (1961a) in his research, as discussed in Chapter 3 and, last but not least, the critical perspective put forward by D. Matza and G. Sykes (Matza, 1961; Matza & Sykes, 1961). With reference to these works, the CCCS's interpretative approach takes a novel angle, focusing on the symbolic dimension and on the concept of *Resistance*.

In creating the theoretical frame of their reflection, Stuart Hall and the young researchers from Birmingham appropriate Phil and Stanley Cohen's previous analyses.

Phil Cohen's (1972) essay on the condition of young people in London's East End offers a pioneering theorisation of the subcultural approach. Cohen reflects on the effects of the urban modernisation project, that kicked off in the 1950s, which he believes to have accelerated the process of social disorganisation and broken down traditions, family relations, the local economy and sense of community in one of the most densely populated areas of the British capital. To pay the price for this process are, according to Cohen, the young offspring of the working-class occupying a liminal position between the class culture expressed by their parents and consumer culture, as advocated by their peers (Brake, 1985; Gelder, 2007). These young people find themselves trapped between the *never again* of the working-class heritage of their ancestors and the *not yet* of the hedonistic image of the affluent consumer hailing from the other side of the Atlantic. Phil Cohen (1972: 59) contends that it is from this unique positioning that youth subcultures emerge in England, as "a compromise solution to two contradictory needs". The latter is a solution that takes on, as will be argued in the next few pages, a predominantly symbolic connotation. In an essay summarising the core tenets of the subcultural approach, Phil Cohen states:

> It seems to me that the latent function of subculture is this: to express and resolve, albeit 'magically', the contradictions which remain hidden or unresolved in the parent culture. The succession of subcultures which this parent culture generated can thus all be considered so many variations on a central theme – the contradiction, at an ideological level, between traditional working-class puritanism and the new hedonism of consumption; at an economic level, between a future as part of the socially mobile elite or as part of the new lumpen proletariat. Mods, parkas, skinheads, crombies, all represent, in their different ways, an attempt to retrieve some of the socially cohesive elements destroyed in their parent culture, and to combine these with elements selected from other class fractions, symbolizing one or other of the options confronting it (*Ivi*: 57, *emphasis in the original*).

Retracing the diachronic sequence along which the different youth subcultures have emerged, Phil Cohen teases out their shared essential features, linked to their being organised around four symbolic subsystems: on the one hand, dress and music; on the other, argot and ritual. From the combination of these subsystems emerge what he calls "cultural structures" able to offer young people who embrace them a new sense of identity – this being expressed in the search for elements of continuity and identification, on the one hand, and of autonomy and difference, on the other, both vis-à-vis the parent culture (a working-class culture), and the dominant culture (a middle-class culture) (Longhurst et al., 1999[3]; Berzano & Genova, 2015). Case in point are the Mods:

> While the argot and ritual forms of mods stressed many of the traditional values of their parent culture, their dress and music reflected the hedonistic image of the affluent consumer (P. Cohen, 1972: 58).

British society reacts to the emergence of urban subcultures with "a wave of hysteria" marred by ambivalence, as "it fluctuates between dread and fascination, outrage and amusement", between the positive acceptance of the innovative thrusts of young people and a concern for the re-definition of cultural and moral boundaries (Hebdige, 1979: 92–93).

In Stanley Cohen's interpretation, this ambivalence evolves itself along a dynamic that gives rise to what he calls the spiral of "moral panic". He defines this concept as follows:

> A condition, episode, person or group of persons emerges to become defined as a threat to societal values and interests; its nature is presented in a stylized and stereotypical fashion by the mass media; the moral barricades are manned by editors, bishops, politicians and other right-thinking people; socially accredited experts pronounce their

diagnoses and solutions; ways of coping are evolved or (more often) resorted to; the condition then disappears, submerges or deteriorates and becomes more visible (S. Cohen, 1972[3]: 1).

In the analysis developed in *Folk devils and moral panics*, with their manner of dress, their way of talking, their music and their fights, the Mods and the Rockers had elicited, in the 1970s, a social reaction that did not limit itself – to quote Howard Becker's model (1963) – to labelling young people as "outsiders", but went one step further, with their collective behaviour becoming a source of "moral panic". Via a jam-packed string of media campaigns, public opinion declared in fact, that those subcultures weren't merely evidence of a behaviour that had to be censored, but also and more importantly, symbolised "the gallery of types that society erects to show its members which roles should be avoided and which should be emulated" (S. Cohen, 1972[3]: 2). As argued by Dick Hebdige (1979: 91–92) subcultures ultimately became an expression of "forbidden contents (consciousness of class, consciousness of difference) in forbidden forms (transgressions of sartorial and behavioural codes, law breaking, etc.)". According to Stanley Cohen, and the CCCS later on, British society had identified young people belonging to youth subcultures as the prime culprits of the decadence of society and its traditional values (Longhurst et al., 1999[3]; Procter, 2004). In other words, they had become the scapegoats of a deep-rooted crisis and an enemy from which society should defend itself (Feixa, 1998[3]).

Differently from the analysis carried out by Phil Cohen, in Stanley Cohen's *Folk devils and moral panics* the roots of youth subcultures remain in the background, to make room for an outlook that revolves around the "reactions" of the world of adults, institutions and specifically, the mass media that "sistematically exaggerate(d) and distort(d) the events" (Longhurst et al., 1999[3]: 326). Mods and Rockers thus become almost "disembodied objects" that "come to life" and are somewhat socially constructed "when their supposed identities had been presented for public consumption" (S. Cohen, 1972[3]: 20), paving the way for social control.

## 5.3. "Resistance through rituals"

Phil Cohen and Stanley Cohen outline the theoretical grounds from which the dense introduction to *Resistance through rituals*, authored by Hall in collaboration with John Clarke, Tony Jefferson and Brian Roberts, takes shape (Longhurst et al., 1999[3]).

Hall and the researchers at CCCS commenced their reflection with a strong critique of the debate on affluence, consensus and embourgeoisement, which had been addressed by the social sciences in the previous decades (Procter, 2004: 86) with an eye to re-*articulating* the class dimension in studies on young people. This allowed them, on the one hand, to critique those perspectives that saw in the rise of "youth culture" a sign of the disappearance of class (Pedretti & Vivan, 2009); and on the other hand, to focus back on the scientific debate on working-class youth, with particular attention – as per the definition employed in the first lines of the essay – to "culture" as a "practice which realises or objectivates group-life in meaningful shape and form" (Clarke et al., 1976[3]: 10). This gave rise, therefore, to what Clarke (2007: 144) has termed as a "double movement", in which "the turn to class is always rendered problematic by the insistence on culture as a privileged site of contestation, where domination and subordination are at stake".

According to the framework set by the "Subcultures Group", to comprehend youth subcultures it is necessary to analyse them within their dialectical relationship with the parent culture – that of the working-class – and the dominant culture. Undoubtedly, they underscore in multiple instances, "sub-cultures must exhibit a distinctive enough shape and structure to make them identifiably different from their 'parent' culture". Furthermore, "they must be focussed around certain activities, values, certain uses of material artefacts, territorial spaces etc. which significantly differentiate them from the wider culture" (Clarke et al., 1976[3]: 13–14). However, youth subcultures reflect and share numerous aspects of the culture of belonging. In a publication that exemplifies the ethnographic nature of their theoretical reflection and writing, CCCS researchers state:

> Members of a sub-culture may walk, talk, act, look 'different' from their parents and from some of their peers: but they belong to the same families, go to the same schools, work at much the same jobs, live down the same 'mean streets' as their peers and parents (*Ivi*: 14).

In other words, youth who participate in British subcultures experience the social and economic contradictions faced by other members of their social class, with whom they share the very same subordinate position in relation to the dominant culture. This coincides, however, with the perception of a generational specificity, that in view of the relationship with consumption and free time, provides young people with a way to stand up to the models imposed by the dominant class and face class-based challenges in a distinct manner from their parents (Brake, 1985; Jenks, 2005).

The cultural practices of Teddy Boys, Mods, Rockers and Skinheads, the subcultures analysed in *Resistance through rituals*, shed light on symbolic expressions that are symptomatic of structural contradictions and mark the consolidation of forms of collective *resistance* to cultural hegemony (Frith, 1984; Williams, 2011). It is thus possible to refer back to Phil Cohen's contention that:

> Through dress, activities, leisure pursuits and life-style, they may project a different cultural response or 'solution' to the problems posed for them by their material and social class position and experience (Clarke et al., 1976[3]: 15).

Each youth subculture is thus understood as an assemblage of different shades of meaning that together make up a "repertoire of strategies" within which the relationship between a fringe of the subordinate class and the dominant culture unfolds: this relationship can express itself along processes of negotiation, resistance or conflict, albeit always in an oppositional sense. Urban youth subcultures are always located – to re-evoke the image put forward by Thrasher (1927[2]) – in an *interstitial* position, namely between parent culture and the dominant culture that they interact with in a direct and pervasive manner in the context of institutions like school, work, leisure time. As CCCS researchers aptly point out, this is not merely about ideological constructs, as subcultures are above all, an attempt to *conquer space*. This space is symbolic and traces the boundaries of subcultural practices: the weekend, clubs, nights spent on the street, soccer games or the "standing-about-doing-nothing" – described by Paul Corrigan (1976[3]) in an essay within the ethnographic section of *Resistance through rituals*. This is also a space wherein to explore new forms of relations, activities, rhythms, activities, sounds, times. It's a space to defend, by drawing boundaries, that once again are symbolic in nature: first of all, the definition of a *jargon* and – as we will see in the next paragraph – of a *style*. All this outlines, according to the "Subcultures Group", "a set of social rituals which underpin their collective identity and define them as a 'group' instead of a mere collection of individuals" (Clarke et al., 1976[3]: 47). Therefore:

> In addressing the 'class problematic' of the particular strata from which they were drawn, the different sub-cultures provided for a section of working-class youth (mainly boys) one strategy for negotiating their collective existence. But their highly ritualised and stylised form suggests that they were also attempts at a solution to that problematic experience: a resolution which, because pitched largely at the symbolic level, was fated to fail (*Ibidem*).

Herein lies the core theory underlying the reflections and ethnographic studies developed in Birmingham: youth subcultures do not solve issues such as educational disadvantage, the reduction of work or unemployment. Thus, it is a process that acts upon the structural roots of class contradictions, without solving them. Rather, subcultures offer youth who become a part of them a symbolic horizon, different from that of their parents, within which they can *re-configure* their experience.

The subcultural response unfolds – as Murdock and McCron (1976[3]) explain – at the intersections of the reproduction of a *consciousness of class* and the emergence of a *consciousness of generation*. In such manner, as Chambers (2013: 68) remarks, "a stepping outside of time and context" takes shape: a dehistoricising of the condition of those subjects that combines the contradictions of classes and generations, leading to their spectacular "explosion". By tracing the boundaries of its symbolic space, youth subcultures give rise, in the CCCS' approach, to their own *resistance* to bourgeois hegemony and the contradictions deriving from their class and generational positioning. At the same time, rehearsing in a *ritualistic* manner their alterity and emphasising the representation of their subordination, they express "a symbolic critique of the established order" (Clarke & Jefferson, 1976: 208). Thus, the theme of the *Resistance through rituals* emerges and in turn influences the key of interpretation that will be used to analyse youth subcultures.

According to the approach employed by the CCCS, the subcultural response should unambiguously be understood "in terms of *lack*" (Gelder, 2007: 90): without embracing those forms of explicit rebellion (Merton, 1949[2]), the emerging solution cannot, thus, impact on the material living conditions of the young people that are part of it (Williams, 2011), nor do the British youth subculture develop into a progressive political movement. To conclude, we can affirm that "such forms of resistance are not necessarily going to 'revolutionise' class structures in the sense of a straightforward inversion; they are *potential forms*" that place the focus on the construction, the adaptation and use of objects and spaces (Procter, 2004: 90). This is an aspect that sets the work of "Subcultures Group" apart from that of Phil and Stanley Cohen to which as we have seen, it was partially inspired, gradually leading the researchers at CCCS to emphasise the expressive and spectacular dimension of youth subcultures (Gelder & Thornton, 1997), to which we now turn our attention.

## 5.4. The meaning of style

Drawing on Jean Genet's (1949) prompts in the *The Thief's Journal*, in one of the most famous analyses produced by CCCS scholars, Dick Hebdige (1979) focuses on the *meaning of style* in the interpretation of youth subcultures. In an autobiographical essay, Hebdige recalls that *Subculture: The Meaning of Style* was written between 1977 and 1978, at the peak of punk in England, and that was commissioned by Terence Hawkes for the "New Accents" series, published by Methuen.

The drafting process of the book gave the then twenty-six year-old Hebdige the opportunity to carry on the research studies commenced in the course of his time at the CCCS, where he had obtained his MA, and "to connect some of the concerns about youth culture, consumption and the politics of insubordination more directly to debates within aesthetics, semiotics, poststructuralism and so forth" (Hebdige, 2012: 400). In the *Introduction* to the book, Hebdige makes clear the perspective at the heart of the analysis:

> we are interested in subculture – in the expressive forms and rituals of those subordinate groups – the teddy boys and mods and rockers, the skinheads and the punks – who are alternately dismissed, denounced and canonized; treated at different times as threats to public order and as harmless buffoons. [...] also, we are intrigued by the most mundane objects [...] which, none the less, [...] take on a symbolic dimension, becoming a form of stigmata, tokens of a self-imposed exile. Finally, [...] we must seek to recreate the dialectic between action and reaction which renders these objects meaningful (Hebdige, 1979: 2).

In his analysis, subcultures represent "texts" to examine with the aid of structuralist and semiotic approaches; while style signifies a space in tension, where objects become the holders of meanings that are always contested:

> On the one hand, they warn the 'straight' world in advance of a sinister presence – the presence of difference – and draw down upon themselves vague suspicions, uneasy laughter, 'white and dumb rages'. On the other hand, for those who erect them into icons, who use them as words or as curses, these objects become signs of forbidden identity, sources of value (*Ivi*: 2–3).

In line with the more general approach to the analysis of subcultures, style itself is understood as a product of the intersection between different elements, responding to different prompts (Frith, 1984). CCCS scholars identify, in first instance, a direct relationship with the practices, the relations, the models, values and the ways of doing of the "parent culture" (Clarke *et al.*, 1976[3]). Other elements are explicitly evoked via symbolic repertoires typical of higher social classes. Others still, are rooted in cultural models typical of other subordinate ethnic groups[1] (Gelder & Thornton, 1997). To these, one should also add,

---

[1] This aspect is particularly important in Hebdige's perspective. In fact, unlike those within the CCCS who had exclusively focused on the class dimension, he delves deeper into the ethnic roots of some subcultural traditions. One should consider, in particular, the reflections made about reggae and rastafarianism, as well as the reading of the style of skinhead and punk.

those elements and activities that are directly connected with the experience of youth: dress, music, jargon; cafes, dance halls, evening outings, soccer games, etc.

Nonetheless, the young people belonging to subcultures apply and transform those elements "to the situations and experiences characteristic of their own distinctive group-life and generational experience" (Clarke et al., 1976³: 53), along a process that denotes new meanings. As John Clarke (1976³) clarifies in a lengthy essay published in the theoretical section of *Resistance through rituals*, the emergence of a subcultural style does not hinge, in fact, on the creation or invention of new objects. Embracing the concept of *"bricolage"* introduced by Claude Lévi-Strauss (1962) in *The Savage Mind*, the researchers at CCCS underscore how the novelty of each style lies, rather, in a mechanism resting on the (active) (re)appropriation of commonly used objects, such as for example a safety pin, shoes, a dress, a motorbike. Just like in bricolage, these objects are, time after time, selected, deprived of their "natural" connotations[2], (re)contextualised and re-combined with other objects, through practices that end up changing and re-constructing their meaning (Brake, 1985; Procter, 2004). In actual fact, the process of re-signification put in place through style can develop along four potential strategies: (a) re-codifying objects from different systems of meaning; (b) modifying or associating in a different way new objects generated or used by a different social group; (c) intensifying, isolating or exaggerating the meaning and value attributed to certain objects; finally, (d) combining different forms according to a "secret" language or code (e.g. a specific jargon) accessible only to the members of the group (Clarke et al., 1976³: 55–56). Hence,

> By repositioning and recontextualizing commodities, by subverting their conventional uses and inventing new ones, the subcultural stylist gives the lie to […] the 'false obviousness of everyday practice' […], and opens up the world of objects to new and covertly oppositional readings (Hebdige, 1979: 102).

Following the chronological sequence of subcultures studied by the British researchers, let's take into consideration four examples (Brake, 1985). First of all, Teddy Boys, the first youth subculture in England, of which the style, as highlighted by a famous *Daily Mirror*'s headline in July 1953, was evident in three factors: *"Flick Knives, Dance Music and Edwardian Suits"*. These were young people dressed in elegant clothes bought in second-hand shops, "suede shoes,

---

2   According to Roland Barthes' analysis, on which CCCS researchers draw, the adjectives indicate that the connotations attributed to objects of the hegemonic culture are perceived by society as the only possible ones, and in this sense "natural" (Clarke *et al.*, 1976³).

velvet and moleskin collars, and bootlace ties" (Hebdige, 1979: 51), who built their social presence by protecting their neighbourhood, engaging in road fights and attacks on Black migrants, considered as the culprits of the disappearance of the working-class world; yet to them they owed their musical tastes, mediated by Elvis Presley and Gene Vincent. A second manifestation is that of the Mods (short for *modernist*), who with their tailor-made suits and home-made shoes exacerbated the premises of social mobility, embodying a style that was so perfect to be considered disconcerting. The third manifestation is that of Skinheads, who, emptying the style of the Mods from every bourgeois tendency, make explicit reference in the construction of their image to the typical traits of the urban proletariat that they proudly represent: shaved hair, well-kept sideburns, bomber jackets, Levi's jeans rolled up to expose their black Dr. Martens (born as working shoes), suspenders and a Ben Sherman shirt or white Lonsdale T-shirt (P. Cohen, 1972). Finally, the *cut up* typical of punks, a subculture which, drawing on and at the same time denying previous subcultures, speaks to the last emblematic manifestation of the process described by the CCCS. The punk style, according to Hebdige's description, manifests itself in:

> a chaos of quiffs and leather jackets, brothel creepers and winkle pickers, plimsolls and paka macs, moddy crops and skinhead strides, drainpipes and vivid socks, bum freezers and bovver boots – all kept 'in place' and 'out of time' by the spectacular adhesives: the safety pins and plastic clothes pegs, the bondage straps and bits of string which attracted so much horrified and fascinated attention (Hebdige, 1979: 26).

Here however it is important to underscore an additional aspect, that becomes particularly relevant in the conceptualisation made by CCCS: to "make the style" are not objects per se, or signs, sounds, words, clothes. Neither is the mere act of using them, playing them, wearing them: "What makes a style is the activity of stylisation – the active organisation of objects with activities and outlooks, which produce an organised group-identity in the form and shape of a coherent and distinctive way of 'being-in-the-world' " (Clarke et al., 1976[3]: 54). To refer to a previously mentioned concept, "it is through stylisation that things are disarticulated from their dominant meanings and rearticulated in new contexts" (Procter, 2004: 92). In order to give life to a different style, objects must, therefore, be decontextualised from their original cultural reference and be collectively re-elaborated and given novel coherence (Berzano & Genova, 2015). Inspired by an interpretation that had been previously suggested by Mungham and Pearson (1976), Murdock and McCron (1976[3]: 203) summarise this process with the following definition:

subcultural styles are the product of a cumulative process of selection and transformation through which available objects, symbols and activities, are removed from their normal social context, stripped of some or all of their conventional connotations and reworked 'by members of the group into a new and coherent whole with its own special significance'.

In his analysis, Hebdige insists on one additional element: in his view, in fact, assigning novel meanings becomes for subcultures a sign of defiance, a rejection, "a crime against the natural order" (Hebdige, 1979: 3), as it breaks the sequence which – according to the connotations of hegemonic culture – normally leads from the signifier to the signified (Berzano & Genova, 2015). Style can thus be interpreted as a struggle within a signification process: a fight between discourse, definitions and values that threatens social and cultural cohesion.

One of the most innovative aspects of the reflection on youth subcultures become apparent: although it originates in the sphere of free time and leisure, within which socio-economic contradictions are less apparent, and that with regard to the "tight discipline of work" is more frequently characterised by a "relative freedom" (Clarke, 1976[3]: 175), style does not simply identify the expressive or playful aspect of subcultures. Rather, it represents the context wherein young people rehearse and perform rituals of resistance towards dominant constructions of meaning. Style thus expresses the context wherein the previously mentioned "symbolic violation of the social order" takes shape (Hebdige, 1979: 19), as a spectacular form through which young people attempt to "embellish", "decorate", make "parody" and thus, "recognize and rise above a subordinate position which was never of their choosing" (*Ivi*: 139). Coming to life is also what Hebdige identifies as a silent shift leading to the overlap – particularly evident in the case of punk – between the image of a "style in revolt" and that of a "revolting style" (*Ivi*: 106 *ff.*): a style, that in other words, is able to engender, as fittingly remarked by Simon Frith (1984: 46), "images which shock not just because they are unusual but because they also threaten the usual stability of imagery".

The next step is that of ascertaining criteria underpinning the birth of a style and the forms of (re)appropriation of the symbolic practices of the marketplace and broader society.

## 5.5. Homology and creativity

In 1978 Paul Willis, one of the first young scholars to join the CCCS, published *Profane culture*, drawing on the research conducted for this PhD dissertation, which he defended in 1972. The research is based on two ethnographic studies conducted in 1969: the first in a motor bike club so as to study a group of young

Rockers; the second near a public house called "The Anchor" to investigate three groups of Hippies. As per other research studies conducted at the time by CCCS, Willis (1978: 1) tasks himself with rendering an account of "the inner meanings, style and movement" typical of the young people he meets.

The peculiar novelty of his work lies in the approach adopted, rooted in the concept of "homology" (Willis, 2000; Sassatelli, Santoro & Willis, 2009): a concept used in *Resistance through rituals* that has been employed at length in the debate on subcultures and, more broadly, in cultural studies (Longhurst et al., 1999[3]; Hughson, 2016). The main objective of his analysis was to identify the type of relationship that comes into being between the sensitivities, the values and the behaviours of the group, on the one hand, and the elements that characterise culture and style, on the other (Brake, 1985). As Willis more recently emphasised, this has allowed him to go beyond a merely descriptive approach, to grasp in which way the motor-bike, the drugs, the musical styles and other typical aspects of the cultures examined "helped to form the whole as material things *and* symbolic things supplying the elements of a cultural meanings system not reducible to them" (Willis, 2014: xxii, *emphasis in the original*). In the "Theoretical appendix" to *Profane culture* he underscores that the central element of his analysis are the so-called "constitutive relationships", namely "the way the social group is connected to the objects, artefacts, institutions and systematic practices of others which surround it" (Willis, 1978: 189). From this perspective, in the *theory of cultural forms* suggested by Willis (1977[2]), the homological level of analysis is specifically orientated to examine, in a qualitative and synchronic perspective,

> how far, in their structure and content, particular items parallel and reflect the structure, style, typical concerns, attitudes and feelings of the social group (Willis, 1978: 191).

It is therefore a matter of ascertaining – as pointed out by Clarke et al. (1976[3]: 56) – the process of recognition and mutual adaptation between cultural objects that make up the definition of a style and the vision of the world of young people who are part of it:

> This involves members of a group in the appropriation of particular objects which are, or can be made, 'homologous' with their focal concerns, activities, group structure and collective self-image – objects in which they can see their central values held and reflected.

In order for this to happen, however, it is necessary that objects possess those that Willis (1978: 200) designates as the "objective possibilities" to "encourage or hold different meanings in different ways", to reflect specific "structures of attitude and feeling", or to "suggest new meanings". In this sense, the concept of homology blatantly expresses that relationship between symbolic aspects of style and – in the CCCS' analysis – the structural roots of urban youth subcultures.

We can thus emphasise that, notwithstanding several internal differences, according to the interpretation of CCCS researchers, the subcultural style is not simply a random conglomerate of different elements. Rather, it is evidence of their combination within an organic whole, that incorporates and expresses the group's self-consciousness (Berzano & Genova, 2015). Thus, the concept of homology allows to shed light on how style offers a form of expression of collective identity that on the one hand, is characterised by the self-representation and self-recognition of members of the subculture, and on the other, is a tool to distinguish one's group from the others, react to their ideas and values, and preserve the boundaries of the group itself.

These observations introduce a second theme developed by Willis in his research on youth subcultures. During an interview with Roberta Sassatelli and Marco Santoro, the British researcher recalled how the ethnographic studies led by the CCCS on spectacular subcultures have also offered the opportunity to explore "alternative ways" through which subjects can appropriate themselves of the commodities and of "the whole variety of things that are produced for profit" (Sassatelli, Santoro & Willis, 2009: 277–278). By comparison with the studies presented in previous pages, Willis emphasises how the practices of young people who belong to the groups examined do not merely represent a ritual of resistance, but have to be interpreted also as forms of social and cultural reproduction and concurrently, potential "catalysts of cultural innovation", on the other (*Ivi*: 265).

In relation to the first point, it is useful to refer back to another ethnography conducted between 1972 and 1975, in the course of which Willis (1977[2]) studied the transition from school to work of 12 working-class lads through their last two years at school and into the early months of work. During his participant observation he noted how the creative and autonomous forms of expression of the cultural style the lads employed in relation to school, teachers and "ear'oles" (read: nerds), there are traces of a silent yet profound continuity with the class culture of their parents, that thus ends up being tacitly reproduced (Dimitriadis, 2008). He maintains, in fact, that those young people are not *forced* to get working-class jobs due to their socio-economic conditions, but rather as a result of complex processes that take shape within working-class culture itself:

> It is here where working class themes are mediated to individuals and groups in their own determinate context and where working class kids creatively develop, transform and finally reproduce aspects of the larger culture in their own praxis in such a way as to finally direct them to certain kinds of work (Willis, 1977[2]: 2).

For them, *Learning to labor* thus represents "an element of self-damnation", which "is experienced, paradoxically, as true learning, affirmation, appropriation" but also "as a form of resistance" by young lads to the socio-economic system (*Ivi*: 3). Once again, this (potentially) bolsters the hypothesis that the subordination and failure of those young people are not inevitable, and that:

> Social agents are not passive bearers of ideology, but active appropriators who reproduce existing structures only through struggle, contestation and a partial penetration of those structures (*Ivi*: 175).

The quoted text re-evokes a typical theme of contemporary sociology (Giddens, 1984), that in Willis takes on a connotation of "*profane* creativity", "the only route – he claims – for radical *cultural* change" (Willis, 1978: 1). Accordingly, in *Ethnographic Imagination* Willis (2000) attempts to emphasise the *dialectical relations* with objects and goods that unfold via the elaboration of styles and meanings. In line with the works of Clarke (1976[3]) and Hebdige (1979), Willis sees in subcultures a specific cultural resource, namely the opportunity to define new stylistic and symbolic codes, which he defines as *"profane power"*. His research allows to ascertain how this power takes shape primarily in everyday life (Williams, 2011), and finds its full expression in all those situations wherein young people – as Paul Corrigan and Simon Frith (1976[3]) point out – live a *material experience* or an intimate involvement with the world. The result is that:

> These cultures work through profane materials: simple functional commodities, drugs, chemicals and cultural commodities exploitatively produced by the new 'consciousness industry'. And yet from the rubbish available within a preconstituted market these groups do generate viable cultures, and through their work on received commodities and categories, actually formulate a living, lived out and concretized critique of the society which produces these distorted, insulting, often meaningless things (Willis, 1978: 3–4).

Willis (2014) has recently argued that what emerges is the plurality of dimensions that shield themselves behind the use of the adjective *"profane"* in his analysis of youth subcultures. As we have pointed out, the objects and materials used by those young people are profane. Their rough, often vandalic life experiences are profane. What is profane, the British ethnographer insists, is even the researcher's attempt to capture through observation, these glimpses of everyday life. Nonetheless, Willis warns (1978: 1), it is precisely this mix of elements that ensures that these "oppressed, subordinate or minority groups can have a hand in the construction of their own vibrant culture", and that the same groups can make use of what he subsequently termed *Symbolic creativity* (Willis, 1990): that is the "qualities, capacities and potentials in those profane things which the dominant society has thrown aside [...] or left undeveloped for cultural meaning" (Willis, 1978: 6).

## 5.6. From symbolic challenges to incorporations

Until now, we have seen that youth belonging to urban subcultures implement ritualistic practices of resistance vis-à-vis the contradictions deriving from their class location and from bourgeois hegemony. We have also mentioned how these symbolic practices take shape primarily within consumer culture and leisure time, along a process of re-appropriation of objects and goods produced by the cultural industry. It should be noted however, that on multiple occasions Birmingham researchers have emphasised the dialectical nature of this process, particularly as regards the dominant culture's commitment to rejecting or re-absorbing young people's creative and symbolic resistance (Williams, 2011).

As argued by Ken Gelder (2007: 94), youth subcultures are, in fact, constantly exposed to the risk that their oppositional strength will be neutralised or of " 'incorporation' back into the dominant system of value and meanings". In relation to the ritualistic practices of young people belonging to the working-class, overt and sometimes tacit mechanisms exist seeking to overcome alterity and heal the symbolic wound that they lament. In noticing the prime role played by the media, Dick Hebdige (1979: 94) articulates the issue as follows:

> Eventually, the mods, the punks, the glitter rockers can be incorporated, brought back into line, located on the preferred 'map of problematic social reality' [...] at the point where boys in lipstick are 'just kids dressing up', where girls in rubber dresses are 'daughters just like yours' [...]. The media [...] not only record resistance, they 'situate it within the dominant framework of meanings' and those young people who choose to inhabit a spectacular youth culture are simultaneously *returned*, as they are represented on T.V. and in the newspapers, to the place where common sense would have them fit [...]. It is through this continual process of recuperation that the fractured order is repaired and the subculture incorporated as a diverting spectacle within the dominant mythology from which it in part emanates: as 'folk devil', as Other, as Enemy.

In the reading of CCCS researchers, the re-arrangement of that *fractured order* follows two different but ultimately converging trajectories. A first one, re-evoked in the closing of the text that has just been quoted, draws on the interpretation lens of "Moral Panics" put forward by Stanley Cohen (1972[3]). Birmingham researchers highlight, in fact, how young people belonging to subcultures are often represented in stereotypical manner by the media, institutions tasked with socialisation and control and through common sense in two ways. In some cases, as "dangerous aliens" and "wild animals" to control and repress;

in others as "boisterous kids" and "wayward pets" whose alterity manifests itself simply at a spectacular level. Both in the first and second case, they claim, their diversity is de-historicised and thus emptied of its power because *too* exotic, trivial and dangerous, or because not exotic, familiar and tameable *enough* (Hebdige, 1979: 97). Thus, "ambivalence […] of the social reaction to youth – patronising publicity and imitation versus moral anxiety and outrage" (Clarke *et al.*, 1976[3]: 74) – re-emerges in all its ideological power.

The second trajectory links back to the processes of *diffusion* and *defusion* of subcultural style described by John Clarke. With the first, reference is made to the broadening of the "cultural space" within which "the selective re-working and re-appropriation of the style by geographically-dispersed groups" can take place. By *defusion* one should intend instead the process through which one style is separated from typical aspects of the subculture which produced it, "dislocated from the context and group which generated it", enhanced with novel meanings through the mechanisms of media enhancement and "taken up with a stress on those elements which make it "a commercial proposition" (Clarke, 1976[3]: 186; 188). At the intersection between these two processes, the subcultural symbols that characterise these relationships, language, clothing and the music of young people belonging to subcultures become once again objects of mass production; the symbolic creativity displayed by the Mods, the Skinheads or the Punks is normalised; the subcultural becomes "trendy", purifying it of all the scandalous elements that could disrupt the social order (Pedretti & Vivan, 2009).

The key elements of the "circular process of subtraction and reabsorption" which, according to the CCCS, govern the antagonistic relationship between subcultures created by working youth and the dominant culture, become apparent (Berzano & Genova, 2015: 141). In fact, if subcultures are born as opposition, defiance, *resistance* to bourgeois hegemony, in a manner that seems paradoxical but ultimately is not, their success is what determines the weakening of their subversive potential and the convergence in the form of goods. A cyclical process, therefore, that transitions between opposition and diffusion, resistance and integration:

> Youth cultural styles may begin by issuing symbolic challenges, but they must inevitably end by establishing new sets of conventions; by creating new commodities, new industries or rejuvenating old ones (Hebdige, 1979: 104).

Herein re-emerge the theoretical underpinnings of the research run by the "Subcultures Group", namely the awareness of the profound power imbalance that governs the relationship between the dominant culture and the symbolic practices of working-class young people. Thanks to an interpretation that is doubtless intellectual indebted to Richard Hoggart (1957[5]), the processes of incorporation and re-absorption that we have described, signifies, time and again "the death of the subculture" (Gelder, 2007: 94).

In actual fact, each integration defines a new balance from which new *fractures* can originate, as well as new rituals of resistance, new processes of bricolage, a new style, therefore – to recall the definition suggested by *Resistance through rituals* – "a different cultural response or 'solution' to the problems posed for them by their material and social class position and experience" (Clarke et al., 1976[3]: 15). In short, it can give rise to the birth of a new subculture. It is precisely around this dynamic that, as discussed in the previous page, the research studies and theoretical elaboration of the CCCS on youth (sub)cultures came to the fore.

## 5.7. Subcultures and beyond

Almost following in the footsteps of Chicago School sociologists, the most intense phase of CCCS' analytical examination of youth subcultures comes to a close swiftly, in less than ten years, closing off in 1979, when Hall transfers to the Open University. In such manner, except for some works – including those of Mike Brake (1985) and Dick Hebdige (1988[2]), even if the latter was already broaching wider topics – throughout the 1980s theoretical and empirical research on subcultures comes to a standstill. The CCCS turns to new themes and analytical frameworks, that are testament to the shift of cultural studies towards an interdisciplinary and innovative approach. Moreover, as Procter argues (2004: 36),

> During the 1980s, the CCCS struggled increasingly to survive as an autonomous Centre and in the late 1980s it was forced to become a department of Cultural Studies offering undergraduate courses. This had a dramatic impact on the nature and capacity of its research and, in 2002, the University of Birmingham made the controversial decision to close the department following a fall in its research ratings.

At the same time, a process of critical reflection and engagement with the body of theoretical, empirical and methodological knowledge gathered by the CCCS arises, also involving those who had played a key role in the "Subcultures Group" (Gelder & Thornton, 1997; Ibrahim & Steinberg, 2014).

From this debate, several problematic aspects, that ought to be recalled, stand out. The first and most well-known, already mentioned by Angela McRobbie and Jennie Garber (1976[3]: 209) in the second part of *Resistance through rituals*, concerns the "quite striking" invisibility of young girls from the literature and the majority of research on youth subcultures in England (McRobbie, 1980; 2008). A second aspect regards the limited attention paid by researchers at CCCS to ethnicity as a potential, autonomous source of forms of cultural and symbolic resistance (Tait, 1992; Dimitriadis, 2008). It is then worth noting the critiques underlining the over-emphasis of the analytical category of class (Middleton, 1990; Redhead, 1990; Wallace & Kovacheva, 1998; Williams, 2011), even in cases where some subcultures appeared to be cross-cutting to the social stratification and many working-class young people did not belong to subcultures (Gelder, 2007). It has also been posited that CCCS researchers may have underestimated youth's progressive process of achieving autonomy from adults (Marsland, 1993). It has been argued that the CCCS somehow "spectacularised" subcultures, all the while neglecting the "ordinary" dimension of young people's everyday life (Frith, 1984; Hughson, 2016), and casual or temporary forms of participation (Gelder & Thornton, 1997).

In a nutshell, the critical re-elaboration of the "classical" subcultural theory of Birmigham's CCCS shows the limits of an essentialist approach (Muggleton, 2000; Sweetman, 2013; Buckingham & Kehily, 2014) that in ways recalls what Dick Hebdige and Stanley Cohen later termed "romanticism" (Muggleton & Weinzierl, 2003). In multiple instances, both the interpretation of the dominant culture and that of subcultures, appear in fact, static and homogenous (Fine & Kleinman, 1979): from this perspective, the need to identify a *subcultural uniqueness* does not allow to grasp the differences emerging from the groups that are analysed time and again, nor the differences between groups. In sum, it can be argued that "preoccupation with theory coincided with a lack of empirical data" (Williams, 2011: 31). Concurrently, subcultures are also considered to have an intrinsic political element, that is not always visible in those who join them (Griffin, 2014). Last but not least, there lacks an adequate attention with respect to the single subjects that initiate those rituals of resistance, meaning the "subjective sense (motivations, points of view, meanings, values) which individuals involved in subcultures assign to their own styles and their own behaviour" (Berzano & Genova, 2015: 130).

It is important to underscore how between the end of the 1970s and the start of the 1980s, the scenario to which Birmingham researchers referred, changed rapidly, reflecting processes that affected the sphere of production (with the decline of the Fordist factory model), social relations, communication, relationships between generations, the market and forms of consumption, modes of expression and representation, the definition of styles (Hodkinson, 2016). Consequently, proletarian subcultures were silently replaced by more fragmented and articulate cultures, in light of new social, economic and political conditions, and in response to the consolidation of novel tools of expression and communication that youth has at their disposal (Pedretti & Vivan, 2009; Buckingham, Bragg & Kehily, 2014).

On the level of theory, this leads to the progressive decline of the reference models of the Marxist and structuralist analyses, replaced with the heterogenous perspectives emerging within social postmodern theory (Bennett, 1999; Muggleton, 2000; Sweetman, 2013). The *post-subcultural turn* which unfolded in the course of the 1990s, is characterised, first and foremost, by the dwindling of two key theoretical tenets of the CCCS: the central role played by class differences and the relevance of the collective dimension of subcultural experience. At the heart of the new approach, there is, instead, the general postulation that social relations, belongings and above all, "youth identities […] had become more reflexive, fluid and fragmented due to an increasing flow of cultural commodities, images and texts through which more individualised identity projects and notions of self could be fashioned" (Bennett, 2011: 493). All the work leading, over time, to the multiplication of the categories used to identify the expressions of the youth is to be intended as part of this trajectory: starting from that of "Post-Subcultures" (Muggleton & Weinzierl, 2003), all the way through the "Neo-Tribes" elaborated by Bennett (1999, 2011) inspired by the works of Michel Maffesoli, to that of "lifestyles" (Miles, 2000) and of "scene" (Straw, 2001; Bennett & Kahn-Harris, 2004; Hesmondhalgh, 2005; Hodkinson & Deicke, 2007), to mention but a few.

It is crucial to highlight how the very same "post-subcultural" paradigm has been the target of criticism (Magaudda, 2009). Re-combining elements typical of sociological analysis with those of cultural studies, some scholars have, in fact, highlighted the – renewed – centrality of two "classical" aspects of CCCS' theory: the first leading back to the possibility of interpreting subcultures as forms, albeit implicit, of collective politically-oriented expression (Blackman, 2004). The second aspect concerns the need to put the focus back on the relation between youth's forms of symbolic expression and the social structure (Shildrick & MacDonald, 2006), made emblematically explicit in the title of the introduction to *Resistance through rituals*, where the connection between "Subcultures, cultures and class" was underlined (Clarke et al., 1976[3]).

Alongside these analyses that, albeit in critical manner, have assumed a subcultural perspective as main reference, it is vital to remember the broader contribution offered by the CCCS to rethinking the *youth question* (Cohen, 1997) and the study of youth cultures (Hodkinson, 2016). To the work of Hall, Jefferson, Hebdige, Willis and the other researchers of the "Subcultures Group" one must give credit for contributing in a substantial manner to introducing new research themes, such as, to make but a few emblematic examples, leisure, loisir, consumption and fashion trends, music, dancing, sports and more recently, digital youth subcultures (Hoskins, Genova & Crowe, 2022). These are themes that have obtained growing centrality in *youth studies*, thus allowing the CCCS' subcultural perspective to take on the traits of a *classical* work with which those who wish to examine youth cultures must take stock.

More generally, also in the light of the critical aspects emphasised above, the analytical pathway developed by the CCCS in the 1970s has brought the attention (back) to the *plurality* charactering youth cultures (Jones, 2009), always seeking – as testified, for instance by the work of Dick Hebdige (Gildart et al., 2020) – to understand social and cultural disruptions as challenges to the orders of normality (Blackman, 2020). A plurality that qualifies and *articulates* in a peculiar manner the approach that Hall and his students have left as their legacy to subsequent generations of scholars. This is particularly relevant as concerns methodological aspects of the research on young people and youth (sub)cultures; the necessity of paying attention to the inequalities and differences that contribute to the definition of young people's life trajectories (first and foremost in terms of social location, gender, generation, ethnic origin); the benefits offered via the adoption of a multi-disciplinary perspective (specifically, cultural studies); finally, the recognition of the multiplicity of experiences, forms of expressions, styles and cultural practices that take shape in young people's everyday life.

As highlighted by Maurice Devlin (2006: 2), the biggest take-away for the social sciences on these themes from CCCS' reflection on subcultures lies, most likely, in the "assault" moved against the *definition* of concepts – that is to the "*thinkability*" of "youth" and "youth culture(s)". In other words, in cases where there is a stiffening of theoretical and methodological positions, there is also the risk of losing sight of the subject of the research: young people, their world and lives (Faeti, 1981).

Starting from this challenge in the following decades, the consolidation of *youth studies* as an integrated and coherent field, yet concurrently open, flexible and aimed to capture the plural forms through which youth cultures manifest themselves, has taken place.

# References

Abbott E. & Breckinridge S.P. (1912). *The Delinquent Child and the Home*. New York: Russell Sage Foundation Charities Publication.

———. (1917). *Truancy and Non-Attendance in the Chicago Schools*. Chicago: The University of Chicago Press.

Abrams P. (1982). *Historical Sociology*. Ithaca: Cornell University Press.

Addams J. (1909). *The Spirit of Youth and the City Streets*. New York: Macmillan.

Allen S. (1968). "Some Theoretical Problems in the Study of Youth". "*Sociological Review*", 16(3), 319–331.

———. (1973). "Class, Culture and Generation". "*The Sociological Review*", 21(3), 437–446.

Anderson M.L. (2008). "Taking Liberties: The Payne Fund Studies and the Creation of Media Experts". In L. Grieveson & H. Wasson (Eds), *Inventing Film Studies* (pp. 38–65). Durham: Duke University Press.

Anderson N. (1923). *The Hobo: The Sociology of the Homeless Man*. Chicago: The University of Chicago Press.

———. (1923/1924). "The Juvenile and the Tramp". In N. Anderson (1998), *On Hobos and Homelessness* (pp. 99–119). Chicago: The University of Chicago Press.

Ardigò A. (1966). "La condizione giovanile nella società industriale". In S. Acquaviva et al., *Questioni di sociologia*, vol. II (pp. 543–613). Brescia: La Scuola.

Arnett J.J. (2004). *Emerging Adulthood: The Winding Road from the Late Teens Through the Twenties*. New York: Oxford University Press.

Attias-Donfut C. (1988). *Sociologie des générations*. Paris: PUF.

Austin J. & Willard M.N. (1998) (Eds). *Generations of Youth. Youth Cultures and History in Twentieth-Century America*. New York: New York University Press.

Bauman Z. (2007). "Between Us, the Generations". In J. Larrosa (Ed.), *On Generations. On Coexistence between Generations* (pp. 365–376). Barcelona: Fundació Viure i Conviure.

Beck U. (2008). "Global Generations in World Risk Society". "*Revista CIDOB d'Afers Internacionals*", 82/83, 203–216.

Beck U. & Beck-Gernsheim E. (2001). *Individualization. Institutionalized Individualism and Its Social and Political Consequences*. London: Sage.

———. (2009). "Global Generations and the Trap of Methodological Nationalism for a Cosmopolitan Turn in the Sociology of Youth and Generation". *"European Sociological Review"*, 25(1), 25–36.

Becker H.S. (1963). *Outsiders: Studies in the Sociology of Deviance*. Glencoe: Free Press.

———. (2008). "Twenty Three Thoughts about Youth". In M.-O. Gonseth, Y. Laville & G. Mayor (Eds), *La marque jeune* (pp. 258–261). Neuchâtel: Musée d'Ethnographie.

Bengston V.L., Furlong M.J. & Laufer R.S. (1974). "Time, Aging, and the Continuity of Social Structure: Themes and Issues in Generational Analysis". *"Journal of Social Issues"*, 30(2), 1–30.

Benjamin W. (1996$^5$). *Selected Writings. Volume 1. 1913–1926*. Cambridge: Harvard University Press.

———. (2011). *Early Writings. 1910–1917*. Cambridge: Harvard University Press.

Bennett A. (1999). "Subcultures or Neo-Tribes? Rethinking the Relationship between Youth, Style and Musical Taste". *"Sociology"*, 33(3), 599–617.

———. (2011). "The Post-Subcultural Turn: Some Reflections 10 Years On". *"Journal of Youth Studies"*, 14(5), 493–506.

———. (2015). " 'Speaking of Youth Culture': A Critical Analysis of Contemporary Youth Cultural Practice". In D. Woodman & A. Bennett (Eds), *Youth Culture, Transitions and Generations: Bridging the Gap in Youth Research* (pp. 42–55). London: Palgrave Macmillan.

———. (2016). *Youth Cultures* (4 Voll.). London: Sage.

Bennett A., & Kahn-Harris K. (2004) (Eds). *After Subculture: Critical Studies in Contemporary Youth Culture*. New York: Palgrave Macmillan.

Bennett J. (1981) *Oral History and Delinquency. The Rhetoric of Criminology*. Chicago: The University of Chicago Press.

Berger B.M. (1960). "How Long Is a Generation?". *"British Journal of Sociology"*, 11(1), 10–23.

———. (1963a). "On the Youthfulness of Youth Cultures", *"Social Research"*, 30(3), 319–342.

———. (1963b). "Adolescence and Beyond. An Essay Review of three books on the Problems of Growing Up". *"Social Problems"*, 10(4), 394–408.

Berger P.L., Berger B. & Kellner H. (1974). *The Homeless Mind: Modernization and Consciousness*. New York: Vintage books.

Bernard J. (1961). "Teen-Age Culture: An Overview". *"Annals of the American Academy of Political and Social Science"*, 338, 1–12.

Berzano L. & Genova C. (2015). *Lifestyles and Subcultures. History and a New Perspective*. New York: Routledge.

Blackman S. (2004). "Youth Subcultural Theory: A Critical Engagement with the Concept, its Origins and Politics, from the Chicago School to Postmodernism". *"Journal of Youth Studies"*, 8(1), 1–20.

———. (2020). "Scavenger and Bricoleur: A Critical Analysis of Dick Hebdige's Repurposing of Subculture Through the Intersection of Biography and History". In K. Gildart et al. (Eds), *Hebdige and Subculture in the Twenty-First Century. Through the Subcultural Lens* (pp. 29–50). Cham: Palgrave Macmillan.

———. (2022). "The Jack-Roller and the Life History Method: Notes on the Chicago School's Clifford Shaw and Howard Becker's Humanistic Narrative of Young Male and Female Delinquents in Different Ages". *"Young"*, 30(3), 213–229.

Blumer H. (1933). *Movies and Conduct*. New York: Macmillan.

———. (1939). *Symbolic Interactionism. Perspective and Method*. Berkeley and Los Angeles: University of California Press.

Blumer H. & Hauser P.M. (1933). *Movies, Delinquency and Crime*. New York: Macmillan.

Bodei R. (2014). *Generazioni. Età della vita, età delle cose*. Bari-Rome: Laterza.

Bourdieu P. (1984). *Questions de sociologie*. Paris: Editions de Minuit.

Brake M. (1985). *Comparative Youth Culture. The Sociology of Youth Culture and Youth Subculture in America, Britain and Canada*. London: Routledge.

Brotherton D.C. & Gude R.J. (2021). *Routledge International Handbook of Critical Gang Studies*. London and New York: Routledge.

Buckingham D. & Kehily M.J. (2014). "Introduction: Rethinking Youth Cultures in the Age of Global Media". In D. Buckingham, S. Bragg & M.J. Kehily (Eds), *Youth Cultures in the Age of Global Media* (pp. 1–18). London: Palgrave Macmillan.

Buckingham D., Bragg S. & Kehily M.J. (2014) (Eds). *Youth Cultures in the Age of Global Media*. London: Palgrave Macmillan

Bulmer M. (1983). "The Methodology of The Taxi-Dance Hall. An Early Account of Chicago Ethnography from the 1920s". *"Urban Life"*, 12(1), 95–101.

———. (1984). *The Chicago School of Sociology. Institutionalization, Diversity and the Rise of Sociological Research*. Chicago: The University of Chicago Press.

Burgess E.W. (1916). "Juvenile Delinquency in a Small City". *"Journal of Criminal Law and Criminology"*, 6(5), 724–728.

———. (1923). "The Study of the Delinquent as a Person". *"American Journal of Sociology"*, 28(6), 657–680.

———. (1929). "Basic Social Data". In T.V. Smith & L.D. White (Eds), *Chicago: An Experiment in Social Science Research* (pp. 47–66). Chicago: University of Chicago Press.

———. (1930). "The Value of Sociological Community Studies for the Work of Social Agencies". "*Social Forces*", 8(4), 481–491.

Buxton W.J. (2008). "From Park to Cressey: Chicago Sociology's Engagement with Media and Mass Culture". In D.W. Parks & J. Pooley (Eds), *The History of Media and Communication Research: Contested Memories* (pp. 345–363). New York: Peter Lang.

Caballero M. & Baigorri A. (2019). "Glocalising the theory of generations: The case of Spain". "*Time & Society*", 28(1), 333–357.

Campbell N. (2000$^2$). "Introduction. On Youth Cultural Studies". In N. Campbell (Ed.), *American Youth Cultures* (pp. 1–29). New York: Routledge.

Canta C.C. (2006). *Ricostruire la società. Teoria del mutamento sociale in Karl Mannheim*. Milan: FrancoAngeli.

Cartosio B. (1992). *Anni inquieti. Società, media, ideologie negli Stati Uniti da Truman a Kennedy*. Rome: Editori Riuniti.

Casavecchia A. (2017). "Connecting Education to Society through Karl Mannheim's Approach". "*Italian Journal of Sociology of Education*", 9(3), 256–264.

Cavalli A. (1994). "Generazioni". *Enciclopedia delle scienze sociali*, vol. 4. Rome: Treccani, 237–242.

——— (2004). "Generations and Value Orientations". "*Social Compass*", 51(2), 155–168.

———. (2020). "Generational Discontinuities and the Memory of Traumatic Events: the Case of Eastern Europe with a Special Focus on Germany". "*European Review*", 28(6), 869–879.

Caygill H. (1998). *Walter Benjamin. The Colour of Experience*. London: Routledge.

Cersosimo G. (2019). *The Making of William I. Thomas: Women, Work and Urban Inclusion. A Social History of Rights and Freedom in the United States at the Beginning of the 20th Century*. Paris: L'Harmattan.

Chambers I. (2013). *Border Dialogues. Journeys in Postmodernity*. Abingdon: Routledge.

Chaney D. (1994). *The Cultural Turn: Scene-Setting Essays on Contemporary Cultural History*. London: Routledge.

Charters W.W. (1933). *Motion Pictures and Youth. A Summary*. New York: Macmillan.

Chicago Motion Picture Commission. (1920). *Report of the Chicago Motion Picture Commission*. Chicago: Chicago Motion Picture Commission.

Chisholm L. (2002). "Mannheim Revisited: Youth, Generation and Life-Course". Paper presented at the ISA XV World Congress of Sociology. Brisbane (Australia), July 7–13 luglio.

––– (2008). "Generations of Knowledge, Knowledge of Generations and the Generation of Knowledge". In R. Rauty (Ed.), *Youth, Control, Citizenship, Social Reproduction* (pp. 159–170). Soveria Mannelli: Rubbettino.

Chisholm L., Kovacheva S. & Merico M. (2011) (Eds). *European Youth Studies. Integrating Research, Policy and Practice*. Innsbruck: M.A. EYS Consortium.

Cicchelli V. & Merico M. (2001). "Adolescence et jeunesse au XX$^e$ siècle. Une esquisse de comparaison entre la tradition sociologique américaine et sa réception en Europe". In INJEP, *Les jeunes de 1950 a 2000. Un bilan des évolution* (pp. 207–230). Marly-le-Roi: INJEP.

Cieslik M. & Simpson D. (2013). *Key Concepts in Youth Studies*. London : Sage.

Clarke J. (1976$^3$). "Style". In S. Hall & T. Jefferson (Eds), *Resistance through Rituals. Youth Subcultures in Post-War Britain* (pp. 175–191). London: Routledge.

–––. (2007). "Introduction". In A. Gray et al. (Eds), *CCCS Selected Working Papers. Vol. 2* (pp. 141–145). London: Routledge.

Clarke J. et al. (1976$^3$). "Subcultures, Cultures and Class". In S. Hall & T. Jefferson (Eds), *Resistance through Rituals. Youth Subcultures in Post-War Britain* (pp. 9–79). London: Routledge.

Clarke J. & Jefferson T. (1976). "Working Class Youth Cultures". In A. Gray et al. (2007) (Eds), *CCCS Selected Working* Papers. Vol. 2 (pp. 200–218). London: Routledge.

Cohen A.K. (1955). *Delinquent Boys. The Culture of the Gang*. New York: Free Press.

Cohen P. (1972). "Subcultural Conflict and Working-Class Community". In P. Cohen (1997), *Rethinking the Youth Question. Education, Labour and Cultural Studies* (pp. 48–63). London: Macmillan.

–––. (1997). *Rethinking the Youth Question. Education, Labour and Cultural Studies*. London: Macmillan.

Cohen S. (1972$^3$). *Folk Devils and Moral Panics. The creation of the Mods and Rockers*. Abingdon: Routledge.

Coleman J.S. (1960). "The Adolescent Subculture and Academic Achievement". "*American Journal of Sociology*", 65(4), 337–347.

–––. (1961a). *The Adolescent Society. The Social Life of the Teenager and Its Impact on Education*. New York: The Free Press.

–––. (1961b). "Athletics in High School". "*Annals of the American Academy of Political and Social Science*", 338, 33–43.

———. (1974). "Youth Culture". In J.S. Coleman (Ed.), *Youth. Transition to Adulthood*. (pp. 112–125). Chicago: The University of Chicago Press.

Coleman J.S. et al. (1966). *Equality of Educational Opportunity*. Washington: U.S. Government Printing Office.

Condliffe Lagemann E. (1994). "Why Read Jane Addams?". In J. Addams, *On Education* (pp. vii–xvii). New Brunswick: Transaction Publishers.

Cooley C.H. (1909). *Social Organization: A Study of the Larger Mind*. New York: C. Scribner's Sons.

Corrigan P. (1976³). "Doing Nothing". In S. Hall & T. Jefferson (Eds), *Resistance through Rituals. Youth Subcultures in Post-War Britain* (pp. 103–105). London: Routledge.

Corrigan P. & Frith S. (1976³). "The Politics of Youth Culture". In S. Hall & T. Jefferson (Eds), *Resistance through Rituals. Youth Subcultures in Post-War Britain* (pp. 231–239). London: Routledge.

Coser L.A. (1971). *Masters of Sociological Thought*. New York: Harcourt Brace Jovanovich.

Côté J.E. (2006). "Emerging Adulthood as an Institutionalized Moratorium: Risks and Benefits to Identity Formation". In J.J. Arnett & J.L. Tanner (Eds), *Emerging Adults in America: Coming of Age in the 21st Century* (pp. 85–116). Washington, DC: American Psychological Association.

———. (2014). *Youth Studies. Fundamental Issues and Debates*. New York: Palgrave.

Côté J.E. & Levine C. (1987). "A Formulation of Erikson's Theory of Ego Identity Formation". "*Developmental Review*", 7(4), 273–325.

Couldry N. (2000). *Inside Culture. Re-imagining the Method of Cultural Studies*. London: Sage.

Cressey P.G. (1932a²). *The Taxi-Dance Hall. A Sociological Study in Commercialized Recreation and City Life*. New York: Routledge.

———. (1932b). "The Social Role of Motion Pictures in an Interstitial Area". "*Journal of Educational Sociology*", 6(4), 231–250.

———. (1934). "The Motion Picture as Informal Education". "*Journal of Educational Sociology*", 7(8), 504–515.

———. (1938). "The Motion Picture Experience as Modified by Social Background and Personality". "*American Sociological Review*", 3(4), 516–525.

———. (1983). "A Comparison of the Roles of the 'Sociological Stranger' and the 'Anonymous Stranger' in Field Research". "*Urban Life*", 12(1), 102–120.

Cristofori C. (1997). *Come nasce un pàradigma. Tra senso comune e scienze sociali. Il caso della giovinezza*, Milan: FrancoAngeli.

Cuzzocrea V. (2018). "Moratorium or Waithood? Forms of Time-Taking and the Changing Shape of Youth". *"Time & Society"*, 28(2), 567–586.

Davis K. (1935). *Youth in the Depression.* Chicago: The University of Chicago Press.

———. (1940). "The Sociology of Parent-Youth Conflict". *"American Sociological Review"*, 5(4), 523–535.

De Martino E. (1961). *The Land of Remorse: A Study of Southern Italian Tarantism.* London: Free Association Books [2005].

———. (1962³). *Furore Simbolo Valore.* Milan: Feltrinelli.

De Maupéou-Abboud N. (1966). "La sociologie de la jeunesse aux Etats-Unis". *"Revue française de sociologie"*, 7(4), 491–507.

De Singly F. (2000). "Penser autrement la jeunesse". *"Lien social et politiques"*, 43, 9–21.

D'Eramo M. (2003). *The Pig and the Skyscraper. Chicago: A History of Our Future.* London and New York: Verso.

Deegan M.J. (1988²). *Jane Addams and the Men of the Chicago School, 1892–1918.* New Brunswick: Transaction Publishers.

Devlin M. (2006). "Editorial. Youth as a Concept Is Unthinkable". *"Youth Studies Ireland"*, 1(1), 2–3.

Dimitriadis G. (2006). "The Situation Complex: Revisiting Frederic Thrasher's *The Gang: A Study of 1,313 Gangs in Chicago*". *"Cultural Studies – Critical Methodologies"*, 6(3), 335–353.

———. (2008). *Studying Urban Youth Culture.* New York: Peter Lang.

Donati P. & Colozzi I. (1997) (Eds). *Giovani e generazioni. Quando si cresce in una società eticamente neutra.* Bologna: il Mulino.

Dubin S.C. (1983). "The Moral Continuum of Deviancy Research". *"Urban Life"*, 12(1), 75–94.

Duffy B. (2021). *The Generation Myth: Why When You're Born Matters Less Than You Think.* New York: Basic Books.

Duncan R. (2013). "The Summer of Love and Protest: Transatlantic Counterculture in the 1960s". In G. Kosc et al. (Eds), *The Transatlantic Sixties: Europe and the United States in the Counterculture Decade* (pp. 144–173). Bielefeld: Transcript.

Dupee F.W. (1968). "The Uprising at Columbia". *"The New York Review"*, September 26 [https://www.nybooks.com/articles/1968/09/26/the-uprising-at-columbia/ – Retrieved: December 2022].

Edmunds J. & Turner B.S. (2002). *Generations, Culture and Society.* Buckingham: Open University Press.

———. (2005). "Global Generations: Social Change in the Twentieth Century". "*British Journal of Sociology*", 56(4), 559–577.
Eisenstadt S.N. (1956). *From Generation to Generation. Age Groups and Social Structure*. New York: Free Press.
———. (1962). "Archetypal Patterns of Youth". "*Daedalus*", 91(1), 28–46.
———. (1971$^3$). "Sociological Analysis and Youth Rebellion". In New Introduction to S.N. Eisenstadt, *From Generation to Generation: Age Groups and Social Structure* (pp. xxv–lxviii). London: Routledge.
Elkin F. & Westley W.A. (1955). "The Myth of Adolescent Culture". "*American Sociological Review*", 20(6), 680–684.
———. (1957). "The Protective Environment and Adolescent Socialization". "*Social Forces*", 35(3), 243–249.
Elster J. (1989). *Nuts and Bolts for the Social Sciences*. Cambridge: Cambridge University Press.
Erikson E.H. (1950). *Childhood and Society*. New York: W.W. Norton & Co.
———. (1963) (Ed.). *Youth: Change and Challenge*. New York: Basic Book.
———. (1968). *Identity, Youth, and Crisis*. New York: W.W. Norton & Co.
———. (1997). *The Life Cycle Completed*. New York: W.W. Norton & Co.
Faeti A. (1981). "Un occhio di riguardo. Viaggio nella giovanologia". "*Inchiesta*", 11(54), 1–11.
Fahlenbrach K., Klimke M. & Scharloth J. (2016). *Protest Cultures: A Companion*. New York: Berghahn Books.
Fass P.S. (1977). *The Damned and the Beautiful. American Youth in the 1920s*. New York: Oxford University Press.
Feixa C. (1998$^3$). *De jòvenes, bandas y tribus*. Barcelona: Ariel.
———. (2020). *Oltre le bande. Saggi sulle culture giovanili*. Rome: DeriveApprodi.
Feixa C. & Leccardi C. (2010). "The Concept of Generation in Youth Theories". "*Revista de Pedagogie*", 58(4), 11–32.
Feixa C., Leccardi C. & Nilan P. (2016) (Eds.). *Youth, Space & Time. Agoras and Chronotopes in the Global City*. Leiden: Brill.
Fields A.B. (1994). "Aperçus du problème des générations: Mentré, Ortega et Mannheim". "*L'Homme et la Société*", 111/112, 7–21.
Fine G.A. & Kleinman S. (1979). "Rethinking Subculture: An Interactionist Analysis". "*American Journal of Sociology*", 85(1), 1–20.
Fishman S. (1975). "Paul Goodman and the Cult of Youth", "*The Educational Forum*", 40(1), 79–85.
Fitzgerald F.S. (1922). *The Beautiful and Damned*. New York: C. Scribner's Sons.

Forman H.J. (1933). *Our Movie Made Children*. New York: Macmillan.

Friedenberg E.Z. (1969). "The Generation Gap". *"Annals of the American Academy of Political and Social Science"*, 382(1), 32–42.

Frith S. (1984). *The Sociology of Youth*. Ormskirk: Causeway Press.

Furlong A. (2013). *Youth Studies. An Introduction*. London: Routledge.

———. (2015). "Transitions, Cultures, and Identities: What Is Youth Studies?". In D. Woodman & A. Bennett (Eds), *Youth Culture, Transitions and Generations: Bridging the Gap in Youth Research* (pp. 16–27). London: Palgrave Macmillan.

———. (2017). *Routledge Handbook of Youth and Young Adulthood*. London: Routledge.

Furlong A. & Cartmel F. (1997). *Young People and Social Change. Individualisation and Risk in the Age of High Modernity*. Buckingham: Open University Press.

Furlong A., Woodman D. & Wyn J. (2011). "Changing Times, Changing Perspectives: Reconciling 'transition' and 'cultural' Perspectives on Youth and Young Adulthood". *"Journal of Sociology"*, 47(4), 355–370.

Galland O. (2003). "Adolescence, Post-Adolescence, Youth: Revised Interpretations". *"Revue Française de Sociologie"*, 44 (Supplement: An Annual English Selection), 163–188.

Geis G. & Dodge M. (2000). "Frederic M. Thrasher and *The Gang*". *"Journal of Gang Research"*, 8(1), 1–49.

Geisshuesler F.A. (2021). *The Life and Work of Ernesto De Martino. Italian Perspectives on Apocalypse and Rebirth in the Modern Study of Religion*. Leiden: Brill.

Gelder K. (2007). *Subcultures. Cultural History and Social Practice*. Abingdon: Routledge.

Gelder K. & Thornton S. (1997) (Eds). *The Subcultural Reader*. London: Routledge.

Genet J. (1949). *The Thief's Journal*. New York: Grove Press [1964].

Gerhardt U. (2002). *Talcott Parsons. An Intellectual Biography*. Cambridge: Cambridge University Press.

Getis V. (1998). "Experts and Juvenile Delinquency: 1900–1935". In J. Austin & M.N. Willard (Eds), *Generations of Youth. Youth Cultures and History in Twentieth-Century America* (pp. 21–35). New York: New York University Press.

———. (2000). *The Juvenile Court and the Progressives*. Urbana: University of Illinois Press.

Giddens A. (1984). *The Constitution of Society. Outline of the Theory of Structuration*. Cambridge: Polity Press.

Gilbert J. (1986). *A Cycle of Outrage. America's Reaction to the Juvenile Delinquent in the 1950s*. New York: Oxford University Press.

Gildart K. et al. (2020) (Eds). *Hebdige and Subculture in the Twenty-First Century. Through the Subcultural Lens*. Cham: Palgrave Macmillan.

Ginzberg E. (1961) (Ed.). *Values and Ideals of American Youth*. New York: Columbia University Press.

Gitlin T. (1972). "Review of *Youth and Dissent*, by Kenneth Keniston". *"Worldview"*, March, 51–53.

Glenn N. (1977). *Cohort Analysis*. London: Sage.

Goodman P. (1960). *Growing Up Absurd. Problems of Youth in the Organized System*. New York: Random House.

———. (1966). *Five Years. Thoughts during a Useless Time*. New York: Random House.

Gordon M.M. (1947). "The Concept of the Sub-Culture and Its Application". *"Social Forces"*, 26(1), 40–42.

Gottlieb D., Reeves J. & TenHouten W.D. (1966). *The Emergence of Youth Societies: A Cross-Cultural Approach*. New York: Free Press.

Gouldner A.W. (1970). *The Coming Crisis of Western Sociology*. New York: Basic Books.

Graham G. (2006). *Young Activists. American High School Students in the Age of Protest*. DeKalb: Northern Illinois University Press.

Gray A. et al. (2007). *CCCS Selected Working Papers* (Volume 1 and 2). London: Routledge.

Grieveson L. (2008). "Cinema Studies and the Conduct of Conduct". In L. Grieveson & H. Wasson (Eds), *Inventing Film Studies* (pp. 3–37). Durham: Duke University Press.

Griffin C. (1993). *Representations of Youth: The Study of Youth and Adolescence in Britain and America*. Cambridge: Polity Press.

———. (2014). " 'What Time Is Now?': Researching Youth and Culture beyond the 'Birmingham School' ". In D. Buckingham, S. Bragg & M.J. Kehily (Eds), *Youth Cultures in the Age of Global Media* (pp. 21–36). London: Palgrave Macmillan.

Habermas J. et al. (1961). *Student und Politik*. Berlin: Luchterhand.

Hall G.S. (1904). *Adolescence: Its Psychology and Its Relations to Physiology, Anthropology, Sociology, Sex, Crime, Religion, and Education*, 2 Vol. New York: Appleton & Co.

Hall S. (1980a). "Cultural Studies: Two Paradigms". *"Media, Culture & Society"*, 2(1), 57–72.

———. (1980b). "Cultural Studies and the Centre: Some Problematics and Problems". In S. Hall et al. (Eds), *Culture, Media, Language* (pp. 2–35). London: Routledge.

———. (1990). "The Emergence of Cultural Studies and the Crisis of the Humanities". *"October"*, 53, 11–23.

Hall S. & Jefferson T. (1976³) (Eds). *Resistance through Rituals. Youth Subcultures in Post-War Britain*. London: Routledge.

———. (2006). "Once More Around *Resistance through Rituals*". In S. Hall & T. Jefferson (Eds), *Resistance through Rituals. Youth Subcultures in Post-War Britain* (pp. vii–xxxii). London: Routledge.

Hall S., Jefferson T. & Clarke J. (1976). "Youth: A Stage of Life?". *"Youth in Society"*, 17, 17–18.

Hall S. et al. (1978). *Policing the Crisis. Mugging, the State, and Law and Order*. London: Macmillan.

Hall S. et al. (1980³) (Eds). *Culture, Media, Language*. London: Routledge.

Hamilton P. (1983). *Talcott Parsons*. London: Routledge.

Hareven T.K. (1976). "The Last Stage: Historical Adulthood and Old Age", *"Daedalus"*, 105(4), 13–27.

Hajdu D. (2001). *Positively 4th Street: The Lives and Times of Joan Baez, Bob Dylan, Mimi Baez Fariña, and Richard Fariña*. New York: Farrar, Straus and Giroux.

Healy W. (1915). *The Individual Delinquent*. Boston: Little, Brown & Co.

———. (1922). *The Practical Value of Scientific Study of Juvenile Delinquents*. Washington: Government Printing Office.

Hebdige D. (1979). *Subculture. The Meaning of Style*. London: Methuen & Co.

———. (1988²). *Hiding in the Light: On Images and Things*. Abingdon: Routledge.

———. (2012). "Contemporizing 'subculture': 30 Years to Life". *"European Journal of Cultural Studies"*, 15(3), 399–424.

Hechinger F.M., & Hechinger G. (1962²). *Teen-Age Tyranny*. New York: Crest Book.

Heer D.M. (2005). *Kingsley Davis: A Biography and Selections from His Writing*. New Brunswick: Transaction publishers.

Helve H. & Holm G. (2005). *Contemporary Youth Research. Local Expressions and Global Connections*. Aldershot: Ashgate.

Hesmondhalgh D. (2005). "Subcultures, Scenes or Tribes? None of the Above". *"Journal of Youth Studies"*, 8(1), 21–40.

Hodkinson P. (2016). "Youth Cultures and the Rest of Life: Subcultures, post-Subcultures and Beyond". *"Journal of Youth Studies"*, 19(5), 629–645.

Hodkinson P. & Deicke W. (2007) (Eds). *Youth Cultures: Scenes, Subcultures and Tribes*. New York: Routledge.

Hoggart R. (1957⁵). *The Uses of Literacy*. New Brunswick: Transaction Publishers.

Hollingshead A.B. (1949). *Elmtown's Youth: The Impact of Social Classes on Adolescents*. New York: Wiley & Sons.

Hollstein W. (1969). *Der Untergrund. Zur Soziologie jugendlicher Protestbewegungen*. Neuwied: Luchterhand.

Hoskins K., Genova C. & Crowe N. (2022). *Digital Youth Subcultures. Performing 'Transgressive' Identities in Digital Social Spaces*. London: Routledge.

Hughson J. (2016). "Ethnography and the Sociology of Culture". In D. Inglis & A.M. Almila (Eds), *The SAGE Handbook of Cultural Sociology* (pp. 294–303). London: Sage.

Ibrahim A. & Steinberg S.R. (2014) (Eds). *Critical Youth Studies Reader*. New York: Peter Lang.

Jahoda M. & Warren N. (1965). "The Myths of Youth". *"Sociology of Education"*, 38(2), 138–149.

Jencks C. & Riesman D. (1968²). *The Academic Revolution*. New York: Routledge.

Jenks C. (2005). *Subculture: The Fragmentation of the Social*. London: Sage.

Johnson R. (1979). "Three Problematics: Elements of a Theory of Working Class Culture". In J. Clarke et al. (Eds), *Working Class Culture: Studies in History and Theory* (pp. 201–237). London: Hutchinson.

Jones G. (2009). *Youth*. Cambridge: Polity.

Jowett G.S., Jarvie I.C. & Fuller K.H. (1996) (Eds). *Children and the Movies. Media Influence and the Payne Fund Controversy*. Cambridge: Cambridge University Press.

Kalmus V. & Opermann S. (2019). "Operationalising Mannheim: Empirical Building Blocks of Generational Identity". *"Comunicazioni Sociali"*, 2, 232–246.

Kecskemeti P. (1952). "Introduction". In K. Mannheim, *Essays on the Sociology of Knowledge* (pp. 1–32). New York: Oxford University Press.

Kelley F. (1889). *Our Toiling Children*. Chicago: Woman's Temperance Publication Association.

–––. (1905). "Child Labor Legislation and Enforcement in New England and the Middle States". *"Annals of the American Academy of Political and Social Science"*, 25(3), 66–76.

Kelly P. & Kamp A. (2015) (Eds). *A Critical Youth Studies for the 21st Century.* Leiden: Brill.

Keniston K. (1960). "The Decline of Utopia". In K. Keniston (1971), *Youth and Dissent: The Rise of a New Opposition* (pp. 27–57). New York: Harcourt Brace Jovanovich.

———. (1962). "Social Change and Youth in America". *"Daedalus"*, 91(1), 145–171.

———. (1962/1963). "The Political Revival". In K. Keniston (1971), *Youth and Dissent: The Rise of a New Opposition* (pp. 81–98). New York: Harcourt Brace Jovanovich.

———. (1965). *The Uncommitted. Alienated Youth in American Society.* New York: Harcourt, Brace & World.

———. (1966). "Faces in the Lecture Room". In R.S. Morrison (Ed.), *The Contemporary University: USA* (pp. 315–349). Boston: Houghton Mifflin.

——— (1968a). *Young Radicals. Notes on Committed Youth.* New York: Harcourt, Brace & World.

———. (1968b). "The University as Critic". In K. Keniston (1971), *Youth and Dissent: The Rise of a New Opposition* (pp. 127–142). New York: Harcourt Brace Jovanovich.

———. (1968/1969). "Drug Users: Heads and Seekers". In K. Keniston (1971), *Youth and Dissent: The Rise of a New Opposition* (pp. 230–252). New York: Harcourt Brace Jovanovich.

———. (1969a). "Counter Culture: Cop-Out or Wave of the Future?". *"Life Magazine"*, 7, November, 8–9.

———. (1969b). "You Have to Grow Up in Scarsdale". In K. Keniston (1971), *Youth and Dissent: The Rise of a New Opposition* (pp. 303–317). New York: Harcourt Brace Jovanovich.

———. (1970). "Idealists: The Perils of Principle". In K. Keniston (1971), *Youth and Dissent: The Rise of a New Opposition* (pp. 253–268). New York: Harcourt Brace Jovanovich.

———. (1971). *Youth and Dissent: The Rise of a New Opposition.* New York: Harcourt Brace Jovanovich.

Keniston K. & Hirsch S.L. (1970). "Dropouts: Development through Discontinuity". In K. Keniston (1971), *Youth and Dissent: The Rise of a New Opposition* (pp. 189–212). New York: Harcourt Brace Jovanovich.

Kerouac J. (1957). *On the Road.* New York: The Viking Press.

Kertzer D.I. (1982). "Generation and Age in Cross-Cultural Perspective". In M.W. Riley, R.P. Abeles & M.S. Teitelbaum (Eds), *Aging from Birth to Death: Volume 2, Sociotemporal Perspectives* (pp. 27–50). New York: Routledge.

———. (1983). "Generation as a Sociological Problem". *"Annual Review of Sociology"*, 9, 125–149.

Kett J.F. (2003). "Reflections on the History of Adolescence in America". *"History of the Family"*, 8(3), 355-373.

Knox G.W. (1991$^5$). *An Introduction to Gangs*. Peotone: New Chicago School Press.

Kontos L., Brotherton D.C. & Barrios L. (2003) (Eds). *Gangs and Society. Alternative Perspectives*. New York: Columbia University Press.

Lapassade G. & Rousselot P. (1998). *Le rap ou la fureur de dire*. Paris: Loris Talmart.

Laufer R.S. & Bengtson V.L. (1974). "Generations, Aging, and Social Stratification: On the Development of Generational Units". *"Journal of Social Issues"*, 30(3), 181–205.

Leccardi C. & Ruspini E. (2006). *A New Youth? Young People, Generations and Family Life*. London: Routledge.

Lesko N. & Talburt S. (2012). *Keywords in Youth Studies. Tracing Affects, Movements, Knowledges*. New York: Routledge.

Lévi-Strauss C. (1962). *The Savage Mind*. Chicago: The University of Chicago Press [1966].

Lifton R.G. (1968). "Protean Man". *"Partisan Review"*, 35(1), 13–27.

———. (1993). *The Protean Self. Human Resilience in an Age of Fragmentation*. New York: Basic Books.

Linton R. (1942). "Age and Sex Categories". *"American Sociological Review"*, 7(5), 589–603.

Lipset S.M. (1968). *American Student Activism*. Santa Monica: Rand Corp.

———. (1993$^2$). *Rebellion in the University*. New Brunswick: Transaction Publishers.

Loader C. (1985). *The Intellectual Development of Karl Mannheim*. Cambridge: Cambridge University Press.

Longhurst B. et al. (1999$^3$). *Introducing Cultural Studies*. Abingdon: Routledge.

Magaudda P. (2009). "Ridiscutere le sottoculture. Resistenza simbolica, postmodernismo e disuguaglianze sociali". *"Studi culturali"*, 6(2), 301–314.

Malin B.J. (2009). "Mediating Emotion: Technology, Social Science, and Emotion in the Payne Fund Motion-Picture Studies". *"Technology and Culture"*, 50(2), 366–390.

Mannheim K. (1928). "The Problem of Generations". In K. Mannheim (1952), *Essays on the Sociology of Knowledge* (pp. 276–322). New York: Oxford University Press.

———. (1929). *Ideology and Utopia. An Introduction to the Sociology of Knowledge*. New York: Harcourt, Brace and Co. [1936].

———. (1935). *Man and Society in an Age of Reconstruction*. London: Routledge & Kegan Paul [1940].

———. (1943). *Diagnosis of Our Time*. London: Routledge & Kegan Paul.

———. (1950). *Freedom, Power and Democratic Planning*. London: Routledge & Kegan Paul.

——— (1952). *Essays on the Sociology of Knowledge*. New York, Oxford University Press.

Mannheim K. & Stewart W.A.C. (1962). *An Introduction to the Sociology of Education*. London: Routledge & Kegan Paul.

Manning P.K. & Truzzi M. (1972) (Eds). *Youth and Sociology*. Englewood Cliffs: Prentice-Hall.

Marcuse H. (1964). *One Dimensional Man: Studies in the Ideology of Advanced Industrial Society*. Boston: Beacon Press.

Marias J. (1949). *El método histórico de las generaciones*. Madrid: Revista de Occidente.

Marsland D. (1993). *Understanding Youth. Issues and Methods in Social Education*. London: Claridge.

Marwick A. (2006). "Youth Culture and the Cultural Revolution of the Long Sixties". In A. Schildt & D. Siegfried (Eds), *Between Marx and Coca-Cola: Youth Cultures in Changing European Societies, 1960–1980* (pp. 39–58). New York: Berghahn Books.

———. ($2012^2$). *The Sixties: Cultural Revolution in Britain, France, Italy, and the United States*. London: Bloomsbury.

Matza D. (1961). "Subterranean Traditions of Youth". *"The Annals of the American Academy of Political and Social Science"*, 338(1), 102–118.

———. (1969). *Becoming deviant*. Englewood Cliffs: Prentice-Hall.

Matza D. & Sykes G. (1961). "Juvenile Delinquency and Subterranean Values". *"American Sociological Review"*, 26(5), 712–719.

Mauger G. (1990). "Postface". In K. Mannheim, *Le problème des génération* (pp. 83–119). Paris: Nathan.

Mayo P. (1990). "Karl Mannheim's Contributions to the Development of the Sociology of Knowledge". *"Education"*, 3(4), 24–30.

McCole J. (1993). *Walter Benjamin and the Antinomies of Tradition*. Ithaca: Cornell University Press.

McRobbie A. (1980). "Settling Accounts with Subculture: A Feminist Critique", *"Screen education"*, 34, 37–49.

———. (2005). *The Uses of Cultural Studies*. London: Sage.

———. (2008). *The Aftermath of Feminism: Gender, Culture and Social Change*. London: Sage.

McRobbie A. & Garber J. (1976³). "Girls and Subcultures: An Exploration". In S. Hall & T. Jefferson (Eds), *Resistance through Rituals. Youth Subcultures in Post-War Britain* (pp. 209–223). London: Routledge.

Mead G.H. (1934). *Mind, Self and Society*. Chicago: The University of Chicago Press.

Mead M. (1928). *Coming of Age in Samoa. A Psychological Study of Primitive Youth for Western Civilisation*. New York: Morrow & Co.

———. (1970). *Culture and Commitment: A Study of the Generation Gap*. New York: American Museum of Natural History, Natural History Press.

Melossi D. (2008). *Controlling Crime, Controlling Society: Thinking about Crime in Europe and America*. Cambridge: Polity Press.

Mercer B. (2020). *Student Revolt in 1968. France, Italy and West Germany*. Cambridge: Cambridge University Press.

Merico M. (2000). *Ernesto de Martino, la Puglia, il Salento*. Naples: ESI.

———. (2002). "Le ossessioni e i silenzi. Per una sociologia della condizione giovanile in Italia". In M. Merico (Ed.), *Giovani come. Per una sociologia della condizione giovanile in Italia* (pp. 1–28). Naples: Liguori.

———. (2004). *Giovani e società*. Rome: Carocci.

———. (2015). "Giovani e processi educativi nelle ricerche di Frederic M. Thrasher". *"Sociologia"*, 49(1), 35–41.

Merico M. & Morciano D. (2017). "Critical Youth Work for Youth-Driven Innovation: A Theoretical Framework.". In S. Bastien & H.B. Holmarsdottir (Eds), *Youth as Architects of Social Change. Global Efforts to Advance Youth-Driven Innovation* (pp. 43–74). Cham: Palgrave Macmillan.

Merton R.K. (1949²). *Social Theory and Social Structure*. New York: The Free Press.

Middleton R. (1990). *Studying Popular Music*. Buckingham: Open University Press.

Miles S. (2000). *Youth Lifestyles in a Changing World*. Buckingham: Open University Press.

Miller T. (2001) (Ed.). *A Companion to Cultural Studies*. Malden: Blackwell.

Milligan I. (2014). *Rebel Youth: 1960s Labour Unrest, Young Workers, and New Leftists in English Canada*. Vancouver: UBC Press.

Mills C.W. (1963). "The Complacent Young Men". In C.W. Mills, *Power, Politics, and People* (pp. 387–394). New York: Ballantine Books.

Mitchell A.M. (1929). *Children and Movies*. Chicago: The University of Chicago Press.

Mitterauer M. (1986). *A History of Youth*. Oxford: Blackwell [1992].

Modell J. (1989). *Into One's Own. From Youth to Adulthood in the United States: 1920–1985*. Berkeley: University of California Press.

Monti D.J. (1993). "Origins and Problems of Gang Research in the United States". In S. Cummings & D.J. Monti (Eds), *Gangs: The Origins and Impact of Contemporary Youth Gangs in the United States* (pp. 3–25). Albany: SUNY Press.

Muggleton D. (2000). *Inside Subculture. The Postmodern Meaning of Style*. Oxford: Berg.

Muggleton D. & Weinzierl R. (2003) (Eds). *The Post-subcultures Reader*. Oxford: Berg.

Mungham G. & Pearson G. (1976) (Eds). *Working Class Youth Culture*. London: Routledge & Kegan Paul.

Murdock G. & McCron R. (1976[3]). "Consciousness of class and consciousness of generation". In S. Hall & T. Jefferson (Eds), *Resistance through Rituals. Youth Subcultures in Post-War Britain* (pp. 192–207). London: Routledge.

Musgrove F. (1964). *Youth and the Social Order*. Bloomington: Indiana University Press.

Nasaw D. (1985[2]). *Children of the City. At Work and at Play*. New York: Oxford University Press.

O'Donnell M. (1985). *Age and Generations*. London: Tavistock.

Ortega y Gasset J. (1923). *The Modern Theme*. New York: Harper [1961].

———. (1933). *Man and Crisis*. New York: Norton & Co. [1958].

Park R.E. (1915). "The City: Suggestions for the Investigation of Human Behavior in the City Environment". "*American Journal of Sociology*", 20(5), 577–612.

———. (1929). "The City as a Social Laboratory". In T.V. Smith & L.D. White (Eds), *Chicago: An Experiment in Social Science Research* (pp. 1–19). Chicago: The University of Chicago Press.

Park R.E., Burgess E.W., McKenzie R.D. (1925$^3$). *The City*. Chicago: The University of Chicago Press.

Parsons T. (1942). "Age and Sex in the Social Structure of the United States". *"American Sociological Review"*, 7(5), 604–616.

———. (1943). "The Kinship System of the Contemporary United States". *"American Anthropologist"*, 45(1), 22–38.

———. (1950). "Psychoanalysis and the Social Structure". In T. Parsons (1954). *Essays in Sociological Theory (Revised Edition)* (pp. 336–347). New York: The Free Press.

———. (1951). *The Social System*. New York: Free Press.

———. (1959). "The school class as a social system: Some of its functions in American society". *"Harvard Educational Review"*, 29(4), 297–318.

———. (1961a). "A Sociologist's View". In E. Ginzberg (Ed.), *Values and Ideals of American Youth* (pp. 271–287). New York: Columbia University Press.

———. (1961b). "Some Considerations on the Theory of Social Change". *"Rural Sociology"*, 26(3), 219–239.

———. (1962). "Youth in the Context of American Society". *"Daedalus"*, 91(1), 97–123.

———. (1989). "A Tentative Outline of American Values". *"Theory, Culture and Society"*, 6(4), 577–612.

Parsons T. & Bales R.F. (1956$^2$). *Family Socialization and Interaction Process*. London: Routledge.

Passerini L. (1997). "Youth as a Metaphor for Social Change: Fascist Italy and America in the 1950s". In G. Levi & J.C. Schmitt (Eds), *A History of Young People in the West. Volume 2* (pp. 281–340). Cambridge: Harvard University Press.

Pedretti R. & Vivan I. (2009). *Dalla lambretta allo skateboard. Teorie e storia delle sottoculture giovanili britanniche (1950-2000)*. Milan: Unicopli.

Pilcher J. (1994). "Mannheim's Sociology of Generations: An Undervalued Legacy". *"British Journal of Sociology"*, 45(3), 481–495.

Pinder W. (1926). *Das Problem der Generation in der Kunstgeschichte Europas*. Berlin: Frankfurter Verlagsanstalt.

Pirni A. (2014). "Disadvantaged Young People, Family and the Lack of Big Brothers. An Interview with Alessandro Cavalli". "societàmutamentopolitica", 5(10), 275–284.

Platt A. (1969$^2$). *The Child Savers: The Invention of Delinquency*. Chicago: The University of Chicago Press.

Podhoretz N. (1967). *Making It*. New York: Random House.

Polan D. (2007). *Scenes of Instruction: The Beginnings of the U.S. Study of Film*. Berkeley: University of California Press.

Popescu A. (2019). "The Brief History of Generation: Defining the Concept of Generation. An Analysis of Literature Review". *"Journal of Comparative Research in Anthropology and Sociology"*, 10(2), 15–30.

Procter J. (2004). *Stuart Hall*. London: Routledge.

Rapson R.L. (1971) (Ed.). *The Cult of Youth in Middle-Class America*. Lexington: Heath & Co.

Rauty R. (1995³). "Uniti nello spirito". In R. Rauty (Ed.), *Società e metropoli. La Scuola sociologica di Chicago* (pp. ix–li). Rome: Donzelli.

———. (2020). "William Thomas and the Growth of American Sociology Between the 19th and 20th Century". *"Italian Sociological Review"*, 10(2S), 369–381.

Redhead S. (1990). *The End of the Century Party: Youth and Pop Towards 2000*. Manchester: Manchester University Press.

Reitman B.L. (1937). *Sister of the Road. The Autobiography of Box-Car Bertha*. New York: Macaulay.

Residents of Hull-House (1895). *Hull-House Maps and Papers*. New York: T.Y. Crowell.

Reynolds M. (1995). *From Gang to Gangsters. How American Sociology Organized Crime 1918–1994*. Albany: Harrow and Heston.

Riesman D. (1950a). *The Lonely Crowd*. New Haven & London: Yale University Press.

———. (1950b). "Listening to Popular Music". *"American Quarterly"*, 2(4), 359–371.

Roszak T. (1969). *The Making of a Counter Culture. Reflections on the Technocratic Society and Its Youthful Opposition*. New York: Doubleday & Company.

———. (1995). "Introduction to the 1995 Edition". In T. Roszak (1968), *The Making of a Counter Culture. Reflections on the Technocratic Society and Its Youthful Opposition* (pp. xi–xxxvii). Berkeley: University of California Press.

Rowntree J. & Rowntree M. (1968). "Youth as a Class". *"Peninsula Observer"*, 2(4), Special supplement, 9–12.

Ryder N.B. (1965). "The Cohort as a Concept in the Study of Social Change". *"American Sociological Review"*, 30(6), 843–861.

Salerno R.A. (2007). *Sociology Noir: Studies at the University of Chicago in Loneliness, Marginality and Deviance (1915–1935)*. Jefferson: McFarland & Company.

Sassatelli R., Santoro M. & Willis P. (2009). "An Interview with Paul Willis. Commodification, Resistance and Reproduction", *European Journal of Social Theory*, 12(2), 265–289.

Schulman N. (1993). "Conditions of their Own Making: An Intellectual History of the Centre for Contemporary Cultural Studies at the University of Birmingham". *Canadian Journal of Communication*, 18(1) [https://doi.org/10.22230/cjc.1993v18n1a717 – Retrieved: December 2022].

Shaw C.R. (1930²). *The Jack-Roller. A Delinquent Boy's Own History*. Chicago: The University of Chicago Press.

———. (1931²). *The Natural History of a Delinquent Career*. Chicago: The University of Chicago Press.

———. (1938). *Brothers in Crime*. Chicago: The University of Chicago Press.

Shaw C.R. & McKay H.D. (1942²). *Juvenile Delinquency and Urban Areas*. Chicago: The University of Chicago Press.

Shaw C.R. et al. (1929). *Delinquency Areas*. Chicago: The University of Chicago Press.

Shildrick T. & MacDonald R. (2006). "In Defence of Subculture: Young People, Leisure and Social Divisions". *"Journal of Youth Studies"*, 9(2), 125–140.

Short J.F. Jr. (1963). "Introduction to the Abridged Edition". In M.F. Thrasher (Ed.), *The Gang. A Study of 1313 Gangs in Chicago (Abridged Edition)* (pp. xv–liii). Chicago: The University of Chicago Press.

Silverstein H. (1972). *The Sociology of Youth. Evolution and Revolution*. New York: Macmillan.

Simmel G. (1911). "The Adventure". In D. Frisby & M. Featherstone (Ed.), *Simmel on Culture. Selected Writings* (pp. 221–232). London: Sage [1997].

———. (1950). *The Sociology of Georg Simmel*. Glencoe: Free Press.

Smith D.M. (1976). "The Concept of Youth Culture. A Reevaluation". "*Youth & Society*", 7(4), 347–365.

Snodgrass J. (1976). "Clifford R. Shaw and Henry D. McKay: Chicago Criminologists". "*British Journal of Criminology*", 16(1), 1–19.

Solomon S.G. (2005). *American Playgrounds: Revitalizing Community Space*. Lebanon: University Press of New England.

Stoehr T. (1990). "Growing Up Absurd–Again". *"Dissent"*, Fall [https://www.dissentmagazine.org/article/growing-up-absurd-again – Retrieved: December 2022]

Straw W. (2001). "Scenes and Sensibilities". *"Public"*, 22/23, 245–257.

Sutherland E.H. & Cressey D.R. (1955). *Principles of Criminology*. Philadelphia: Lippincott.

Sweetman P. (2013). "Structure, Agency, Subculture: The CCCS, Resistance through Rituals, and 'Post-Subcultural' Studies". *"Sociological Research Online"*, 18(4), 227–236.

Tait G. (1992). "Re-Assessing Street Kids: A Critique of Subculture Theory", *"Youth Studies Australia"*, 11(2), 12–17.

Tenbruck F.H. (1965). "Formal Sociology". In L.A. Coser (Ed.), *Georg Simmel* (pp. 77–96). Englewood Cliffs: Prentice-Hall.

Thomas W.I. (1921²). *Old World Traits Transplanted*. Montclair: Patterson Smith.

———. (1923). *The Unadjusted Girl: With Cases and Standpoint for Behavior Analysis*. Boston: Little, Brown & Co.

Thomas W.I. & Thomas D.S. (1928). *The Child in America. Behavior Problems and Programs*. New York: Knopf.

Thomas W.I. & Znaniecki F. (1918/1920). *The Polish Peasant in Europe and America. Monograph of an Immigrant Group*. Boston: The Gorham Press.

Thorpe C. & Inglis D. (2019). "Do 'Global Generations' Exist? From Mannheim to Beck and Beyond". *"Youth and Globalization"*, 1, 40–64.

Thrasher M.F. (1926). "The Gang as a Symptom of Community Disorganization". *"Journal of Applied Sociology"*, 1(1), 3–27.

———. (1927²). *The Gang. A Study of 1313 Gangs in Chicago*. Chicago: The University of Chicago Press.

———. (1928). "The Study of the Total Situation". *"Journal of Educational Sociology"*, 1(8), 477–490 and 1(10), 599–612.

———. (1936). "The Motion Picture: Its Nature and Scope". *"Journal of Educational Sociology"*, 10(3), 129–142.

Touraine A. (1974²). *The Academic System in American Society*. New Brunswick: Transaction publishers.

Turner B.S. (1999). *Classical Sociology*. London: Sage.

Wallace C. & Kovacheva S. (1998). *Youth in Society. The Construction and Deconstruction of Youth in East and West Europe*. London: Macmillan.

Walton D. (2008). *Introducing Cultural Studies. Learning Through Practice*. London: Sage.

Weber M. (1904). *The Protestant Ethic and the Spirit of Capitalism*. New York: C. Scribner's Sons [1930].

White L.D. (1929). "The Local Community Research Committee and the Social Science Research Building". In T.V. Smith & L.D. White, (Eds), *Chicago: An Experiment in Social Science Research* (pp. 20–32). Chicago: The University of Chicago Press.

Whyte W.F. (1943²). *Street Corner Society. The Social Structure of an Italian Slum.* Chicago: The University of Chicago Press.

Whyte W.H. Jr. (1956). *The Organization Man.* New York: Simon and Schuster.

Widmer K. (1980). *Paul Goodman.* Boston: Twayne Publishers.

Williams J.P. (2011). *Subcultural Theory: Traditions and Concepts.* Cambridge: Polity Press.

Williamson H. (2017). *Supporting Young People in Europe. Looking to the Future.* Strasbourg: Council of Europe Publishing.

Willis P. (1977²). *Learning to Labor: How Working Class Kids Get Working Class Jobs.* New York: Columbia University Press.

———. (1978). *Profane Culture.* London: Routledge & Kegan Paul.

———. (1990). *Common Culture: Symbolic Work at Play in the Everyday Cultures of the Young.* Buckingham: Open University Press.

———. (2000). *The Ethnographic Imagination.* Cambridge: Polity Press.

———. (2014). "Moment. Preface to the 2014 Edition". In P. Willis (Ed.), *Profane Culture* (pp. xi–xxvi). Princeton: Princeton University Press.

Wilska T.-A. (2017). "Youth and Generations in Consumption". In M. Keller et al. (Eds), *Routledge Handbook on Consumption* (pp. 314–325). Abingdon: Routledge.

Wirth L. (1938). "Urbanism as a Way of Life". *"American Journal of Sociology"*, 44(1), 1–24.

Woldring H.E.S. (1986). *Karl Mannheim. The Development of His Thought.* New York: St. Martin's Press [1987].

Wolff K.H. (1971) (Ed.). *From Karl Mannheim.* New York: Oxford University Press.

Woodman D. (2015). "Using the Concept of Generation in Youth Sociology". In A. Lange et al. (Eds), *Handbuch Kindheits- und Jugendsoziologie* (pp. 1–12). Wiesbaden: Springer NachschlageWissen.

———. (2016). "The Sociology of Generations and Youth Studies". In A. Furlong (Ed.), *Routledge Handbook of Youth and Young Adulthood* (pp. 20–26). London: Routledge.

Woodman D. & Bennett A. (2015a). "Cultures, Transitions, and Generations: The Case for a New Youth Studies". In D. Woodman & A. Bennett (Eds), *Youth Culture, Transitions and Generations: Bridging the Gap in Youth Research* (pp. 1–15). London: Palgrave Macmillan.

———. (2015b). "Transitions, Cultures, and Future of Youth Research". In D. Woodman & A. Bennett (Eds), *Youth Culture, Transitions and Generations: Bridging the Gap in Youth Research* (pp. 186–191). London: Palgrave Macmillan.

———. (2015c) (Eds). *Youth Culture, Transitions and Generations: Bridging the Gap in Youth Research*. London: Palgrave Macmillan.

Woodman D. & Wyn J. (2014). *Youth and Generation. Rethinking Change and Inequality in the Lives of Young People*. London: Sage.

Wyn J. & Cahill H. (2015) (Eds). *Handbook of Children and Youth Studies*. New York: Springer.

Wyn J. & White R. (1997). *Rethinking Youth*. London: Sage.

Yinger M.J. (1960). "Contraculture and Subculture". "*American Sociological Review*", 25(5), 625–635.

Young K. (1931). "Analysis 37: Frederic M. Thrasher's Study of Gangs". In S.A. Rice (Ed.), *Methods in Social Science. A Case Book* (pp. 511–527). Chicago: The University of Chicago Press.

Zorbaugh. (1925). "The Natural Areas of the Cities". In E.W. Burgess (Ed.), *The Urban Community* (pp. 219–229). Chicago: The University of Chcicago Press.

———. (1929$^2$). *The Gold Coast and the Slum. A Sociological Study of Chicago's Near North Side*. Chicago: The University of Chicago Press.

www.ingramcontent.com/pod-product-compliance
Ingram Content Group UK Ltd.
Pitfield, Milton Keynes, MK11 3LW, UK
UKHW021823140426
5217IPUK00004B/61